How to Co-Parent With An Abusi
and Keep Your Sanity
(Or at least try)

By Julie Boyd Cole,
Domestic Abuse Survivor, Mother, Co-parent, Advocate and Journalist

Dedication

This book is dedicated to my children, who inspire me every day;

To the victims who face an enormous, life-altering challenge in this troubling age of abusers co-parenting with their victims;

And to the women who have lost their lives and their children because of domestic abuse.

In Memory

Of my Mom, Ginny Bull, who taught me many things, but most importantly what it means to set boundaries and what happens if you don't.

Acknowledgments

I would like to thank Sarah Jane Brownell for editing this book under a tight deadline and her loving support through it; Nancy Boyd and Denver Fredlund for their input and review of this work and continued love; and Jessica Goldberg for her review of my work and suggestions, and her efforts in my emotional health after abuse. I would also like to thank Rosa Boyd and Robin Doxey, who both supported me with their time and advice along the way. I would like to thank the attorney who helped me through the turbulent waters of a custody suit, Elizabeth Martin. Lastly, I would like to thank the women who have shared their stories with me. I cannot give them personal acknowledgments because they must remain anonymous to protect their children from courts and abusive co-parents. They are my inspiration.

Table of Contents

To Begin, A Message from the Author

How to co-parent with an abusive ex and stay sane _ is that even possible?

What's next, "How to lose weight without dieting or exercising?" Sure, whatever. If I overeat and sit around all day, I'm not going to lose weight.

How does anyone co-parent with an abusive ex and stay sane? Simple, don't co-parent with an abusive ex.

Frankly, if you have that choice, take it. It's the best option.

Abusers abuse and divorce doesn't stop their need. If you share children together, you will always be an easy target.

However, most of us don't have that choice. Since the mid-1990s, family courts believe abusers have the right to parent their children, and children have a right to be parented by abusers _ because the abuser is a parent.

To make matters worse, most family courts don't want to hear too many details about the abuser's actions. Nor do parenting coordinators or attorneys. Even family and friends don't want to know. Maybe even your children don't want to know.

I didn't either and I was the victim.

Abuse is painful and hard to look at, especially when we are invested in the abuser. No one wants to see the ugliness of domestic abuse. Why would we? Abusers look normal enough that we marry them. We build a life with them. Trust them. Love them. Then at some point, they pull the rug out from under us.

They show their true colors and rip us apart. Who wants to see that.

The day I married my abuser, we stood together on a sunny beach before our family to recite our vows. I had such stage fright that I gave my vows to the Justice of the Peace to read. My abuser, dressed so beautifully in a fresh pressed suit, not only read his, but read to me one of the most lovely paragraphs anyone has ever said to me. He wrote it himself. I was moved and felt appreciated and loved.

Less than a year later, he had his hands around my neck squeezing tight and I struggled for my life.

Why would I want to face that.

Denial feels so much better. That is what kept me with my abuser for 15 years. I wasn't in a complete fog. I knew his violence had to stop for us to be happy.

In those 15 years, I worked hard trying to find the cure that would stop my ex from physically hurting me, psychology damaging me and messing with my head. I wanted to stay with him. Yep, that sounds crazy. But, a lot of the time, he didn't beat me up. In fact, the majority of the time I wasn't getting physically assaulted. There were even pieces of my life with an abuser that I loved. I loved being married, having children, being a stay-at-home mother. I loved the lifestyle. I loved having a companion. I loved sharing my children with their father. I loved holidays and spending time with our friends. I loved a lot about my life with my abuser.

I hated the abuse. I was scared and so confused.

In the 15 years I was with my abuser as his girlfriend, fiancee and wife, I saw seven different therapists, read at least a dozen relationship books, had hundreds of hours of "come to Jesus" conversations with my abuser, all in an effort to stop the abuse and live a happy life.

I worked so hard at trying to solve this problem so that we could once and for all put an end to the violence and get busy raising our children together.

Time and time again, I applied the methods of pop psychology or a Sunday sermon or advice from Oprah. I listened intently to anything that came my way that seemed like it might help.

But, he kept hitting me.

Over the years, the few therapists I told that there was domestic violence in our home, told me the only way to stop the violence was to call the police or leave.

Call the police? Really? How was that going to help, I thought. Sure, he would stop hitting me that moment, but our relationship would be blown up, too. I didn't want that. I wanted my happy home.

Society was also telling me to call the police and get away with my kids. "Leave as fast as you can with nothing but the clothes on your back." The conventional wisdom at the time: Get to a domestic abuse shelter. Ok, say I did that, then what? You want an unemployed housewife to choose homelessness for me and my kids? Wow, what a great option.

I didn't want any of that. I just wanted him to stop hitting me. I didn't want my kids to be homeless. I didn't want my kids to be without a father. I didn't want a divorce. I wanted the man on the beach who stood next to me promising his eternal love.

But, abusers abuse and no matter how they dress up, there is ugliness inside.

So, I finally took the only action that made him stop hitting me. I left. I gave up all the good things that I loved about being married to the father of my children because if I didn't pull myself out of denial and get out, I would have died or gone truly crazy. I chose life and sanity.

At first, I was applauded for leaving by those who knew about the abuse. I was told I made the right decision to get away from an abuser and save my kids. I was applauded, at first.

But, life after I left didn't solve everything for everyone.

Old habits die hard.

Where I couldn't create a happy marriage with my abuser, I tried to create a friendly divorce. He found new ways to abuse that didn't require being in the same home with me. I tried to figure that out, too. More therapy, books and advice from others. More long conversations. More denial.

When our divorce escalated to obvious abuser/victim dynamic all over again, I blamed myself again, got therapy and tried to build boundaries between us and keep my distance. I was already divorced, but we were parenting together. I tried to instill over and over distance and rules to keep him away from me.

But this time, no applause by the onlookers.

This time I was told by lawyers, a mediator, a parent coordinator and even some friends and family to ignore the abuse and just try to find a way to get along with him for the kids sake.

"What the hell do you think I've been trying to do for 15 years," I thought. "Do you think that I don't know I would have been better off if I could have found a way to just get along? Do you think I wanted to be beaten, strangled, lied to, abandoned, blamed, harassed, spit on, insulted, manipulated, divorced, financial strapped and sued for custody of my children?"

I read every book and spent thousands on mental health's finest. Tried all the advice and even tried to come up with my own ideas.

"Tell me, please, what have I missed?" I thought whenever someone tried to give me well meaning advice. "What exactly do you want me to do, because if you have the magic pill that will help me to 'just get along' then for God's sake, give it to me. I'll take it. Will that make the abuse stop?"

First, I was judged for staying, now I'm judged for trying to get away.

However, I know those judging folks didn't understand what 15 years of trying to "just get along" with an abuser does to a person. I have a lot of anger, sadness and pain for what my abuser stole from me.

But, too many people confidently served up that advice and held back their compassion. Because after all, despite all the "You are not to blame" campaigning, apparently, I was to blame.

It's enough to make a person insane.

Abusers abuse.

Being in the same orbit with them, means that you are in danger of being abused.

Most abusers only abuse their intimate partners _ not their co-workers, friends or even strangers on the bus _ because they can get away with abusing their loved one. If my abuser did what he has done to me to his co-worker, he'd be fired. If he did it to a stranger on the bus, he'd be arrested and jailed.

But, because he did it to me _ his wife, then ex-wife _ well, that's different. Society doesn't like dealing with that scenario so much. Families should handle those cases. We don't like dirty laundry between two consenting adults. None of our business.

It's no wonder our society wants victims to figure out a way to get along with their abuser and co-parent. As if it were that easy.

I have not found a single mental health expert who will say that co-parenting with a domestic abuser is good for children, the family or even society. Children raised as witnesses to abuse grow up with higher rates of all sorts of psychological damage and sociological issues.

I have not found a single mental health expert in domestic abuse who says that an abuser can stop abusing without having had years of therapy and intervention programs. Even then, the odds are against it.

I have not found a single study that shows that co-parenting is the ideal choice when one parent is a domestic abuser.

If you have, send it to me. I would love to see it.

However, there is plenty out there that says domestic abusers should not be co-parenting.

For example, in the family law statute in Florida, domestic abuse is listed as one reason of just a handful, when a judge can rule that one parent be aware sole custody.

One domestic abuse advocate said it best with this post *http://www.katelinmaloney.com/blog/domestic-violence-should-abusers-co-parent.* To sum it up, abusers have shown by their choice to abuse their partner that they cannot be trusted to put the best interest of the children above their needs.

Dr. Rick Nauert, who has over 25 years experience in clinical, administrative and academic healthcare, wrote an article for PsychCentral about this topic and said family courts that force co-parenting between abuser and victim are forcing victims into dangerous situations. (*http://psychcentral.com/news/2006/10/06/co-parenting-with-an-abusive-ex/310.html*)

The University of Illinois studied child custody after domestic abuse and found a lot of mental turmoil as a result of the continued contact victims have with their abuser. *(http://faculty.spokanefalls.edu/InetShare/AutoWebs/kimt/co-parenting%20with%20abusive.pdf)*

"Joint custody can be quite beneficial to the children of these non-violent, low-conflict couples, but not in cases of battering," reported the National Online Research Center for the Violence Against Women organization. http://www.vawnet.org/applied-research-papers/print-document.php?doc_id=371 *The VAWnet.org is supported by grant number 5U1VCE001742-03 from the National Center on Injury Prevention and Control/Centers for Disease Control and Prevention (NCIPC/CDC).*

In this study, they found that children living with one parent who abuses struggle in many ways, no matter whether the parents are divorced or not.

There is this study conducted in 2002 with findings on how abusive men parents. In a nutshell, not very well. *(http://www.lfcc.on.ca/HCT_SWASM_13.html)*

So, with so much evidence building that says abusers should not be co-parenting with anyone, why are so many victims forced to do so?

According to a national survey I conducted in 2015 of victims of abuse who share children with their abuser, 97 percent are co-parenting with their abuser and the large majority of them are continuing to be abused post divorce.

Abusers abuse. We know that. It has been proven. Abuse is a life choice by the perpetrator. They are not driven by the circumstance except in this one way: Give an abuser the opportunity to abuse when he needs to feel the power of abuse, and he will abuse.

How can you co-parent with that?

You shouldn't have to. But, unfortunately, the vast majority of family court judges are awarding shared custody to abusers and victims every day. Even victims of abuse are allowing co-parenting for the same reasons they stayed with their partner during abuse. They hope they can "just get along" and provide the best childhood for their children.

How can you co-parent with your abusive ex and stay sane. Well, the truth is, it isn't easy and sometimes you can't stay sane through this. But, I know from my own experience and the experience of others that with life hacks, resiliency and your undying love for your children, you can maintain your sanity and even thrive through this craziness.

Though I know that this book doesn't give you the real, direct answer you want _ to avoid co-parenting with your abusive ex_ I hope it will give you solid tips to help you get through this nightmare without losing your sanity forever.

The Playing Field
What the Hell is Going On?

In a 2015 national survey of domestic abuse victims, only 8% reported that the abuse stopped after divorce.

And 70% of those divorced, domestic abuse victims, are currently sharing custody of their children with their abuser.

I was first physically abused by my husband when I was almost nine months pregnant. While I sat in a the glider rocker my grandmother gave me as a shower gift, he attacked me during a pretty low-key argument about something I can't remember. He charged at me from the other room, wrapped his hands around my neck and squeezed, pinning me against the high-back seat of the rocker. He made grunting sounds as he squeezed. Thankfully and despite my giant pregnant stomach, I was able to awkwardly get my feet up and push him off me using the momentum of the rocker to give me the necessary power. He fell back, then ran from our home. At that moment, I became one of 37 percent of pregnant women who are battered by their partners. *(Psychology Today)*

The next 10 years of our marriage was filled with violence, arguing, lying and abandonment. And yet, I didn't realize I was married to an abuser and that I was a typical domestic abuse victim. Instead, I thought I was in a volatile marriage with a troubled man and I was a strong, smart women who could help him live a better life. I was loyal and clinging to the fantasy that we could get through this. Eventually, we could provide a happy life for our children. We just hadn't found the right formula.

Sadly, I was wrong.

According to the National Domestic Abuse Hotline, 1 in every 4 women will become the victim of severe physical abuse. Once physical violence has been introduced into an intimate partner relationship, it tends to become the norm. According to the The House of Ruth, a Maryland domestic abuse victims support agency, physical violence almost always increases in severity and frequency. Abusers seek methods to gain power and control over their world as a coping skill for their inner fear and insecurities and when violence works to overpower their intimate partner, they will use it again.

I believed for a very long time, that the struggles of marriage and an imperfect union drove the violence I suffered. If I got out of the marriage, then the abuse would end, I thought.

I was wrong about that as well.

The United States Department of Justice describes intimate partner abuse like this:

"We define domestic violence as a pattern of abusive behavior in any relationship that is used by one partner to gain or maintain power and control over another intimate partner. Domestic violence can be physical, sexual, emotional, economic, or psychological actions or threats of actions that influence another person. This includes any behaviors that intimidate, manipulate, humiliate, isolate, frighten, terrorize, coerce, threaten, blame, hurt, injure, or wound someone."

When I learned the full definition of domestic abuse, I realized that even after divorce, I was still its victim. My ex-husband continued to bombard me with demands, threatening emails, insults, false accusations, and one of the most painful hurts ever bestowed on a mother _ he unsuccessfully sued me for custody of our then teenagers, five years after our divorce.

I learned that domestic abuse doesn't stop at the steps of divorce court.

It is hard to find statistics on the type of abuse victims face after they have ended a relationship with partners hell-bent on power and control. Our society is just coming to terms with the criminalization of intimate partner physical abuse and why it is everyone's problem to solve. Just a few decades ago, husbands were legally allowed to physically assault their wives, control their finances and even rape them. It has taken millions of dollars, years of campaigns and legislation state by state to change the laws and allow partners to call the police when assaulted by their loved-one.

Too many people today, including police officers, judges, legislators and lawyers, believe that ending the relationship ends the abuse. Unfortunately, that is not always the case. When an abuser-victim union produces children, the relationship doesn't end after the break-up because the two parents will always have their children connecting them.

At the same time, family courts have been awarding shared, 50/50 custody in most cases based on the premise that children have a Constitutional right to be parented by both people and that parents have the right to be parents. This ethos is nothing to do with what is the best interest of children. Family courts around the country do not allow the victim to keep the children away from the abuser and leave the relationship with sole custody. In fact, family court most often insists that victims forget about the abuses of the marital relationships and ignore any further attempts of abuse by their former partners.

The "No-fault" divorce movement of the 1970s established that the reasons for divorce are the business of the couple and not the court's, so the process begins "blind." Family courts recognize both victim and abuser coming through the door as equal and entitled to have custody of the children.

This evolution has created a conflict between criminal and family courts and poses the question: If victims are not to be blamed for domestic violence and are not to be held responsible in criminal court, then why are judges in family court doing the opposite? Why are the reactions of abused victims being treated equally as the destructive actions of abusers?

Though people abuse for a variety of reasons, those who have a pattern of exploiting loved ones are often operating under a emotional cloud developed in a damaged childhood that leads to a self-centered approach to life and burning need to "win" in relationships. Simply, abusers abuse as a way to soothe their emotional pain and instability. Often, abusers are not even aware that what they are doing is wrong. They believe that they are entitled to maintain the upper-hand in the relationship and they believe they are successful when they do so. By maintaining control, they get what they want and believe it makes them "winners" when they do, no matter the cost. *(www.StopAbuseCampaign.com, David M. Allen, M.D., University of Tennessee and "How Abusive Men Parent" http://www.lfcc.on.ca/HCT_SWASM_13.html)*

Divorce doesn't end that need.

In the 2015 national survey I conducted, I asked those who were co-parenting after domestic abuse several questions because I wanted to find out if others were experiencing abuse post-divorce (or break up). I was shocked at results.

Of the 87 people who responded anonymously from 30 states, Canada, Australia and Hong Kong, 90 percent reported that the abuse hadn't stopped after the relationship ended. These victims are still dealing with all manners of abuse post-divorce and much of it is legal in the United States. Those actions that are not legal, like assault, harassment, threats and exploitation, often are not reported by the victims. Civil violations, like slander, are complicated and expensive for victims to litigate. As is the case during the unions, victims still don't report most of what is happening against them for all the same reasons they didn't report the abuse when they were married.

Another alarming statistic gained from the survey, 98% responded that their children had witnessed the post-divorce abuse and yet only 25 percent of these children had received therapy.

Those facts are troubling to a parent trying to remove their children from the trauma and turmoil of an abusive home. It is even more staggering when you think about the studies that show how devastating and life-altering witnessing domestic abuse is to a child. Study after study reveals that children in an abusive family start life with a number of strikes against them, not the least of which is that they unfortunately believe that domestic abuse is acceptable.

When I decided to leave my abusive husband, I did it because I wanted to provide a better life for my children and I believed that getting them out of such a volatile household would give them the best chance of a normal childhood. I had finally given up on the fantasy of a two-parent home. I decided that a peaceful, safe home would be the next best thing. I envisioned the end of the chaos of power and control that drove our daily lives. I believed that I could set us all on a better, straighter path, driven by love, respect and understanding.

But, like 90 percent of those who responded to my survey, domestic abuse still directed much of our lives after divorce.

Here are the numbers pulled from my Google Forms survey:

Respondents: 95% were women and 96% of their abusers were men; 99% said they were victims of domestic abuse; 100% said they were no longer in the relationship and they shared children.

70% of respondents said they now share physical custody of their children and just about half said their abusers have physical custody of their children more than 30% of the time.

So, despite domestic abuse in the home before divorce, the majority of abusers had been awarded physical custody of at least 30 percent of their children's time and in some cases, full custody. I knew from my own custody case that it was very possible for a family court system to dismiss domestic violence as relevant evidence in deciding what is best for the children, but I had no idea how common this was.

"I truly thought I was escaping a bad situation when I finally left, but I wasn't. I'm still in an abusive relationship," one responder said.

"The courts rejected my restraining order because he's 'only' been violent once since I left him even though it was in front our daughter," another woman said.

It was true that courts around the land were telling victims to ignore the abuses of the past and co-parent with their abusers. I have since learned through research that even women who were victims of rape can be forced by courts to share custody with their rapists.

"I don't know why the judges can't see … the abuse, bullying, control and harassment just continues through the court," one responder said.

"No one seems to care about the truth. My judge actually said she didn't want to hear any further testimony because it's all 'he-said-she-said' to her even though I had a witness," another woman said.

How is this even possible or good for children? It is impossible for me to understand how judges believe that it is even psychologically possible for a victim of abuse to remain emotionally healthy enough for the daily ups and downs of parenting if they are forced to stay in contact with their abuser. How does anyone believe that this is safe or that it doesn't open up the family for further abuse.

I asked in the survey to check off the type of abuses these victims suffered before divorce and after divorce. Almost 70 percent had been hit, grabbed or pushed by their now co-parent partner during their union. Almost 30 percent had been choked or injured with a weapon and 56 percent of these abusers had threatened violence against the responders. The survey showed that these victims experienced all manners of emotional and physiologic abuse as well, such as lies and manipulation to financial and employment control, to social life and family control. Of the respondents, 71 percent said their abusive partners devalued and discredited them to their children or attempted to turn the children against them.

And 74 percent of the abusers threatened their victims with a custody suit.

Despite a long list of abuses used by one partner against the other, the majority of these people were awarded overnight, weekly time with their kids and the right to be a full participant in the parenting decisions. Imagine how these victims feel each night that their babies are taken away from them and legally put in the hands of someone they know is dangerous.

It boggles the mind.

In my survey, 95 percent of responders said they believe family courts in America need reform and only 30 percent were satisfied with the ordered custody arrangement.

So, why does this happen in the United States today? Well, in part it may be that family court judges don't want the burden of investigating the parenting skills of each parent. Evidence-based trials take a lot of time. Court dockets are already insanely overcrowded. Cases get knocked off a lot quicker when victim and abuser start on a level playing field. Partly, it may be that our society doesn't truly understand domestic abuse and the dynamics involving child custody.

But, the survey I conducted might suggest another reason. Of the responders, only 46 percent even presented domestic abuse as evidence in family court regarding child custody at the time of the divorce. Of those who didn't, 17 percent were advised by their attorneys not to and another 17 percent never got the chance because of the "no-fault" divorce status.

"The judge admitted she didn't read any documents during our hearing," said one responder.

"It's impossible to prove emotional abuse in court," said another.

And in the cases where domestic abuse was introduced, only 32 percent were investigated by any law enforcement, judge or third party advocate.

Domestic abuse just isn't taken as seriously in family court as the numbers show that it should and family court officials are more apt to believe that two fighting parents are equally to blame for the current predicament. I interviewed one family court judge in Florida about his views about child custody cases and he said that the better parents don't sue each other for custody of their children. They don't need a court order to do what is best for their children, he said. This thought process sets up victims in court because it takes only one parent to sue the other, but once again victims are blamed for their abusers' actions.

"There is a massive disconnect in family court regarding violent men and their ability and willingness to 'parent' or 'co-parent' and cooperate in a non-abusive manner," said one responder to the survey.

According to a study released by the Department of Justice in 2011, most family court professionals are not trained in domestic abuse and how family court is being used by abusers. It also showed that these professionals are innately biased against the women who claim to have been abused.

The study was conducted by Dr. Daniel Saunders *(https://www.ncjrs.gov/pdffiles1/nij/grants/ 238891.pdf)* and the University of Michigan and funded by the Department of Justice. They found that most child custody case professionals, such as attorneys, judges and family evaluators are not properly trained in the dynamics of domestic abuse and the coercive control of the abuser.

As a result, a high number of victims are put back in danger, children are put in the care of the abuser and some victims are loosing total custody of their kids.

My survey of victims also shows that most of this group of abusers found a safe haven to control their victims post-break up in the family court system. Abusers are allowed to file as many motions and court actions as they wish against their former spouse. Just like physical violence, once the behavior is introduced into the relationship and it provides a payoff for the abuser, it is likely to continue, no matter how damaging it is to the defendant or the innocent children.

Of those who responded to my survey, almost all experienced continuing harassment and third-party intervention post-divorce in the form of family court motions, interaction with parenting coordinators or mediators, or police called to the scene by the abuser. One responder said she had been living a decade of post-divorce hell thanks to repeated family court motions filed by her ex-husband. Even though she has physical custody of her now teenagers, her ex-husband has filed almost a dozen motions against her for a variety of reasons in two separate states. Her six-figure retirement account has been drained on legal fees. She has had a series of lost jobs and no longer works in her profession. She lost her home and more importantly, her confidence. She receives very little child support because her wealthy ex has hidden money. Her children have had their share of troubles as well that have caused her enormous emotion pain and anxiety. Today, she counts down the days when her youngest child will be 18, when she hopes the legal abuse will end.

Through all of this repeated legal haggling, her abuser sends her demanding and accusatory emails, refuses to give her his address or even report what state he calls his residence, and though he rarely sees his children, he insists on maintaining control of his court-ordered visitation schedule. Because he has the right to "hold" holidays, vacation time and weekends as his parenting time, she is unable to plan ahead and then must adjust if he chooses to cancel the visit. For several years now, her ex sees very little of the children, just a few weeks a year, yet by court order, she must maintain the schedule and keep him in the loop on all parenting decisions. As a result, her abuser continues to control her daily life.

All attempts she has tried to reason with her abuser and encourage him to tamp down emotional flare-ups over minor issues and work together in the best interest of their children, only seem to fuel his willingness to battle over everything and engage with her from a win-lose point of view.

Another respondent of my survey said simply this, "I feel like my children and I have been robbed of a normal, healthy mother and children relationship by the actions of my ex and the legal system he has used against me and that has let him get away with it."

Psychologists are just beginning to study the effects all of this continued battling has on victims and the children. I haven't found one yet that indicates that victims and children are not seriously traumatized and scarred by this form of power and control. But, if these actions were taking place between two non-related adults, then charges of extortion and harassment, both felonies, would be investigated by police, state attorneys and grand juries.

The experts in the field of domestic abuse do advocate that people can stop or at least reduce domestic abuse if abusers are held accountable and given immoveable boundaries, especially if the abuser has a personality disorder, such as narcissism. I often imagine my abuser as a toddler having a temper tantrum when I need perspective to navigate life with an abuser as a co-parent. Like toddlers, they need someone they accept as their authority to tell them to stop the behavior, not help them rationalize or deflect responsibility.

In my opinion, this is how family court judges drop the ball. In their understandable efforts to remain impartial and fair to both parties _ defendant and plaintiff _ they are missing the opportunity to actually stop abuse and protect children's childhoods. Some abusers will immediately stop using an abusive coping skill if an authority figure in their life tells them it is wrong and they will be punished if it continues. Give an abuser even the hint that their victims might play a role in the broken relationship, and you have given an abuser the license he seeks to use the horrible skill. It might be too simple to say that abusers abuse because they are allowed to and because they believe that their victims have earned it, but, I haven't seen any evidence to the contrary. *(To read more about how abusers think, go to* peacefulpaths.org *)*

So, what the hell is going on? We are living in an age when knee-jerk legislation to solving broad problems is the norm and leaders are trying to right the wrongs fathers have faced in decades past when mothers were given full custody of children regardless of circumstances. Our systems are over-taxed and stretched thin. Our media jumps from headline to headline trying to gain a crowd the fastest rather than go in-depth on stories. We have all come to believe that problems can be solved with quick, simple solutions every time. We live at a time when one-size-fits-all is a lot easier to maintain than the more complicated issues that take educated, smart, professional approaches.

In order to fully protect victims and children from further abuse through co-parenting orders, a lot of work needs to be done. In the individual cases, judges and evaluators need to actually investigate domestic abuse allegations thoroughly and weigh claims against what they understand as norms and expected behaviors. Lawyers need to do a better job of helping victims win necessary boundaries between the abuser and the victim that go beyond restraining orders. Legislators need to create laws that identify and criminalize all coercive behaviors in domestic relationships just as they have criminalized such behaviors between strangers.

It is un-Constitutional in the United States to attempt to control the actions of another, especially using intimidation. Too often we somehow believe that after marriage and divorce, that basic principle doesn't apply to victims in abusive relationships. Becoming a family doesn't mean that each has signed over their human rights to their partner or parent.

We still struggle with this and we aren't there yet. So, despite the insanity of trying to cooperate and communicate with the person who beat you, choked you, stabbed you, raped you, terrorized you, and belittled you in order to get you to do what he wants, you are most likely stuck having to figure out how to do this without losing your mind or your children.

It sucks.

But, there are steps you can take that will make it at least manageable. Hang in there. It does get better. You have a very difficult journey, but there are those of us on the other side who can encourage you to find the path that works best for you. Reach out. Speak up and let the world know that you are doing your best in a ridiculous situation.

I offer my story as a way to maybe help you find yours.

These steps within are not the only answer to your problem, or even everything you can do. But, these steps mattered for me during my journey through co-parenting with my abuser.

Step 1

Grieve the Loss of the Fantasy Family

When I was nine years old, my parents divorced after a troubled marriage. My brother and sister and I were very hurt, but not surprised. I was raised in a very typical WASPy, multi-generation family during the 1960s and '70s. My parents' divorce was the first one I knew about among my friends, certainly in my family, and happened at the start of the women's liberation, Free-to-Be-You-And-Me era. I didn't know it, but we were ahead of the curve of the broken family statistics, not the odd balls.

But, at the time, as a little girl, the divorce made me different. As my parents began to make new lives for themselves after divorce, my brother and sister and I tried to find our place in these new worlds and grieved the loss of our family. We never really figured it out. Not my parents and not us. In the end, we all craved forevermore that lost home life.

As I entered adulthood, I secretly feared that I would never be good enough to find someone who would want what I wanted: to get married; have children; and create that family that I had longed to have again. I fell in love several times in my early years, but mostly without telling the guy I loved him. I remained aloof for reasons only my therapist can understand, who of course sees it clearly. I still don't.

As a result, my romantic life before I married was not that fantastic or even romantic. The one time in my early years that I actually loved the man I was with, who said he loved me too, burned out quickly. I was frozen in fear just about every day with him because I was afraid that I would loose this undeserved gift. That didn't make for a healthy relationship and he eventually gave up trying to open me up and moved on.

Unfortunately, my early experiences created the belief in me that relationships and family structures are fragile and can be taken away.

When I met my husband, I was far enough down the road of child-bearing years and I was beginning to panic that my dream of children, the white picket fence equipped with the rocking chairs and my fantasy husband wasn't going to come true.

He was not that attractive and I wasn't attracted to him. He was smart as hell and somewhat witty. He made me smile more than he made me laugh. I met him at work so I knew his co-workers and his reputation. It was so-so. He was the kind of guy that you would hear others crack jokes about, and not flattering jibes. But, he was good at his job and dedicated. I believed he had a good work ethic and that counted with me.

He also came on strong from the first day we met. I'm not sure why, but he immediately showed his interest in me and that blinded me to the red flags that were flying everywhere. One enormous flag I ignored was that he had a girlfriend. I never met her and he rarely talked about her, but when he did, he painted a picture of a shrew who he was continuing to date because he felt sorry for her. He said they always knew they wouldn't be together forever because she didn't want to have children. I believed him and allowed myself to dismiss that relationship.

For weeks we flirted and he showed me a side that I didn't think others saw. At the time, I chalked up the criticism I heard about him to misunderstandings and idle gossip. To me, I saw the good in him. I liked very much that he seemed to like me.

Fairly soon after I met him and despite his girlfriend, we began an on-again, off-again relationship that we kept secret from our co-workers. As time went on, I began to communicate my desire for a family. He showed interest, but toyed with me on the subject. One minute he said he wanted children, the next he wasn't sure.

He also told me often that he was about to break it off with his girlfriend once and for all. He told me that again and again. Months went by and he was still seeing us both. Our relationship progressed forward anyway and finally he asked me to move in together. He reported that he had broken off for good his relationship with his girlfriend and was ready to commit to me exclusively.

Rather than be suspicious or intolerant of such a shady romance, I was elated. I remember the first time he told me he loved me, I was in tears but not because I was in love with him. I was in love with the idea that someone loved me, someone wanted to be with me and start a family.

Of course, I completely missed that he was lying. He hadn't really broken it off with his girlfriend. Once she found out about me, she became the mistress that I once was. At some point in the future, it ended. After we divorced, he told me that he was juggling his college sweetheart and a new woman for more than two years and it was getting hard to handle. So, I guess, when I think back on my relationship with him, I never really knew whether I was the only one.

So began our journey together. Every milestone we reached was shaky and not on a firm foundation. We got married. Ten months after our wedding date, our first son was born. The physical abuse had started just one month before his birth, but I ignored it. Nothing could shake my excitement to have a family, finally, at age 31. My eye was on the fantasy.

Our life continued in marriage for another 10 years, filled with all forms of abuse found on the power and control wheel (http://www.ncdsv.org/images/powercontrolwheelnoshading.pdf) and when there was a particularly rough spell, I made an appointment with yet another marriage counselor. We went through, either together or apart, seven of them in 11 years. No one was able to tell me how to fix this bad marriage. I was angrier and angrier that no one could help me have the fantasy I longed for or how to keep my marriage together.

That didn't stop me from constructing the rest of the elements of the traditional American family. We had another child, bought a house, rescued a dog and I gave up my career and became a stay-at-home mother. I was in the PTA, hosted giant Christmas parties. We joined the local Presbyterian church and held barbecues on the weekend.

Not one month went by in all those years without me getting secretly hit, pushed, choked, stomped on, thrown, kicked, spit on, abandoned or lied to behind our closed front door. I was told often that I was to blame, worthless, the reason for the violence and abuse.

As the years past, I spent more and more time submitting to the physical abuse because I knew the fight would end quicker if I did.

After a few days of emotional recovery, we would open our front door to our family and friends and start over. Our secret safely tucked away in our own collective memory.

However, it became harder and harder to ignore how horrible our marriage was and how horrible I felt. I used all my emotional efforts to maintain my denial. I desperately wanted my marriage to this man, the father of my children, to work out. I wanted those rocking chairs on the porch and the grandchildren playing in our front yard. I wanted my family back.

I fought hard to keep my fantasy going. I was able to ignore that I was a domestic violence victim and the vulnerability that I could be killed at any time. I was able to pretend to all my family and friends that though our marriage wasn't perfect, it was normal and good. We even avoided telling most of our therapists what was really going on.

A few years before divorced, I told our marriage counselor for the first time that he was hitting me. It turned out that she was not equipped to deal with such a revelation and immediately asked me "Why didn't you call the police?" I am sure she was in shock at this disclosure considering we had for weeks sat on her sofa talking about mundane subjects like household duties and communications issues. She wasn't expecting to hear this. My husband had been hanging his head as I told the story of the abuse and when her first words were to me and not him, his head immediately snapped up and he turned and said to me, "Yeah, why didn't you call the police?" He had been handed a way to skirt responsibility right there in the therapist's office and blame me again.

It was the first time I ever experienced victim shaming by society, but hardly the last.

I was in no condition to tolerate this and through anger and tears, I got up and left rather than answer the question. The therapist followed after me sputtering words of comfort that were of no help.

A few months later, we tried it again with new therapist. This time my ex was sent to anger management and a batterers intervention support group. He continued to hit me through it all.

Despite this, we tried to have more children. I had three miscarriages. We went deep into the process of adopting a child from India. My beloved mother was diagnosed with breast cancer and eventually died at 63 years old. We bought a new house and moved again. He lost his job once and got another. I went back to work as a part-time real estate agent. Our life moved on, but with more and more tension and strife.

Maybe because I had excellent grief therapy when my mother, my best friend, died or maybe I was just getting older, I started to face the reality that my husband was never going to stop and our marriage would never change. Our children were getting older and in elementary school and were more aware of the anger and violence. My mother's death was a wake up call in many ways. First, I was dangerously obese due to comfort eating through my traumatic marriage. I decided to put an end to that and took dramatic steps with the help of doctors and took off more than the 100 pounds I had put on during my marriage.

I began exercising and seeing a therapist again. I also began working more regularly with a lot of financial success. My husband didn't seem interested in me and spent more and more time away from home, traveling for work and he began to sleep in another room.

My life was actually beginning to look better though, thanks to my new perspective about mortality and death. I had not yet given up on my marriage, but it was becoming clear to me that I could "fix" myself all I wanted, but unless he fixed himself, I was going to continue to get hit and never really be healthy.

One day, I sat on the sofa of my new therapist's sofa crying and angry. I was so mad because I absolutely knew that these emotional experts had to have the formula to fix this broken marriage and stop the violence in my house. But they, for some reason unknown to me, wouldn't tell me.

I told my therapist, "Just tell me how I can make him stop hitting me, damn it!"

She calmly took a breath and said, "You're right. I haven't told you. I'm sorry. I will tell you now."

I was so relieved. Finally, finally, finally I was going to get the information I needed to have the life I wanted. My happy-ending was just a few words away. I sat up and readied to learn the secret to a better marriage.

"You have two choices and only two to stop him from hitting you," she said and then continued. "One. You must accept him for exactly who he is. That means that no matter what he does or says to you, you must accept it. You may not argue with him about anything. You must do as he asked. You must go where he wants to go. You must leave him alone when he wants to be left alone. You can not have any expectations of him, ever. You can never correct him or tell him that he is not meeting your needs. Don't get angry around him and don't lose it."

I looked at her like she was increasingly crazy. What, I can't do that, I thought. I know that he says I am demanding, but I can't completely bury everything I want or need. That would suck. I can't accept all that he does to me and our kids. I want him to be a better father. I knew that I wasn't even sure I liked him anymore. Basically, she was telling me I would have to completely hide all my "negative" emotions all the time, while he should be allowed to any emotions he wanted. No, that didn't seem fair or realistic. I would have to go with the second option and I waited impatiently for her to tell me.

"Or," she said. "You have to leave him." And then there was silence.

Her words landed hard, but the second she said them, I got it. The first option was not an option I could manage, let alone live with, nor could most people. Sure, there were victims out there who tried to live that life and those victims were dying a slow death in the process, in my opinion.

More importantly, in my fantasy family life, I never envisioned life as a doormat, ghost of a human being, living only to please my husband. We were partners, equally respectful of each other and each other's desires and needs. We were examples for our children and a picture of a healthy marriage. It may have been unrealistic, but what she proposed looked nothing like happiness to me.

"Ok," I said. "I got it. I have to leave him."

That began my journey to start my life over, at age 41, with two children, a part-time job and years of domestic violence under my belt.

I began to accept the truth about my marriage and my husband. As I write this, I can still feel the pit that formed in my stomach that day. It wasn't easy to come out of years of denial. He didn't seem to want to change the status quo and made no real efforts to do so.

On that day, my lifelong fantasy died.

Accepting my options was the first step to grieving the loss.

It took many years and hours and hours of excellent therapy for me to see my life for what it was and to realize that the early picture I painted for my life wasn't going to happen. I was not in control of that. Even if I never divorced my husband in an attempt to keep it together for appearance sake only, there is no guarantee that he would have stayed with me. Abusers don't value people, even people in their own family.

Once I began to look at the variables in my life for what they really were instead of what I wanted them to be, I began to heal.

I've read about and even experienced the five stages of grief in my life before and I realized I needed to grieve again. I had to literally mourn the loss of my dream to live to a ripe old age with the father of my children and never give my kids the experience that I had a as a child of divorce. I had to mourn that I could not control that outcome.

Grieving, crying, pleading with God, getting angry are all important emotional steps to getting to emotional health after trauma. Divorcing an abuser isn't easy. I needed, and my kids needed, my emotional health. There were going to be pitfalls in the road ahead.

The process of grief is so important to me now that I have literally tackled it like a kitchen recipe:

How to Achieve Emotional Health After Deep Emotional Pain

1 Hour of crying over the truth (if you can't muster tears on your own, play sad movie like Steel Magnolias or sad music to trigger tears) Repeat as often as necessary until the tears naturally stop flowing

1 Hour of daydreaming for a miracle to change the truth

1 5-page letter to my ex, written and then thrown out, calling him out for all that he has done to me and the kids

Watch upbeat movie about someone's triumph over adversity, like HBO's *The Crash Reel* or *Touching the Void* (found on Netflix)

Mix all ingredients together, which could take up to several days, maybe even weeks.

You will know when your grief is done when you can smile again and can get out of bed on time and take care of daily responsibilities.

Also, if you can manage it, take a few sick days at work in order to give yourself enough, unscheduled time to cry.

I have used this recipe over and over again through the years and especially after the horror of a custody suit. With the help of my excellent trauma treatment therapist, a social worker named Jessica, I am better able to navigate the slings and arrows my abuser still throws at me from time to time.

I have learned that I can't control what the court orders me to do in raising my children or how my abuser interacts. I can't stop my ex from abusing me. I can't even stop myself from the reaction common to those of us with PTSD. I also can't give my children what I desperately wanted to give to them: a childhood without divorce or pain caused by an abusive parent. I don't have that power.

I can't have the white picket fence with the rockers on the porch and grow old with the father of my children. That fantasy isn't real. My life isn't on that path.

I love the movie *The Crash Reel,* the documentary about Olympic hopeful Kevin Pearce, who was headed to the 2010 Winter Olympics as a snowboarder. He was on a winning streak, beating the top contender Shaun White and was about to make history, when during a practice run, he fell in the bowl and slammed his helmeted-head hard against the frozen snow. He was in the hospital for months, suffered a severe head injury and never competitively snowboarded again. Shaun White went on the win the Olympic Gold and stayed atop the leaderboard for years.

The Crash Reel story begins just before the accident because the filmmakers happened to be on the mountain making a documentary about the snowboard community. The crew caught everything on video.

I believe that though the story is tragic and the crash is horrible, it was a gift to people like me. Because over the course of two years, the film crew documented Kevin's recovery and his grieving process at the loss of what could have been if only he hadn't hit his head that day.

I cried a lot the day I watched it. He was just a kid, a teenager, when this all happened. It took him a very long time and the amazing support of his family to move through the recovery, the grief and a new beginning. He had to let go of his lifelong dream, even though he was so close to achieving it, and move on.

I emailed Kevin to thank him for sharing his story with the world. Because that movie truly showed me that I was a bit like Kevin. I had a childhood dream that I was so close to achieving, too. But, circumstance didn't provide me the opportunity, just like Kevin. *(http:// kevinpearce.com/)*

I was ready to create a new dream. One that would be good for my children and me. It was time to see a new life chapter and adventure.

From now on, I accept that I can only do my best when life throws a curve.

When my reactions are less healthy than I would like, I forgive myself and accept that I am not perfect. Tomorrow will be another day.

I may not pull off this new way of thinking like that amazing snowboarder, but I was going to try, and I told Kevin that in my email.

He wrote me back and thanked me and his encouragement meant a lot to me. I will be forever grateful that young man shared his story with the world.

If you are reading this, then you are likely a victim of an abuser who is trying to mess with your life because doing so makes him feel powerful. Likely, you have been racking your brain, trying to figure out how you can get through to him. I'm also betting that you are tired and may be ready to throw in the towel, anything just to get him to stop causing you and your children so much pain.

I am so sorry. I don't have to know you or know specific circumstances, to know completely that it is not your fault. No one can do anything to make another person abuse someone. That is always the abusers choice. I'm here to tell you, you can not fix that in him. There is nothing you can say, or do, or not do, or not say, or act in just the right way that will bring out the best in him.

However, abusers will always make you think that you can. Abusers will tell you one day that you deserve his horrible treatment because of some supposed transgression on your part. Then the very next day, they can brush the whole infraction under the rug as if he never really cared. Then the next minute, he can change his mind again. Essentially, no matter what you do, you are not safe until he seeks real help from a domestic abuse counselor and completely and always absolves you of blame for his abuse.

You are not in control of that. Only he can make that choice.

So, grieve the loss of the fantasy of the family you wanted, or the positive and fair divorce you tried to give to your children. Through grieving, you will begin to move on and find a new normal for you and your children.

Step 2

Get Emotional Help

One thing I trust about everyone in the world, is that we all want to be happy. We may not always do the things that we need to do to get there, but we want it anyway.

It is very difficult to live a life of happiness when there is someone in your world who will exploit you, use you, scare you and cause you all other forms of hurt.

Co-parenting with an abuser is the act of sharing your most treasured gift from God with likely the only person on the planet who will actively try to hurt you.

How can anyone live happily with this black cloud hanging over? How is this not a hopeless situation?

Well, from my experience, sometimes I feel exactly that way and it is very difficult to see an end to this turmoil.

But, stories like Kevin Pearce's remind me that all people collect challenges, pain and disappointment in life and can still live a life of joy. Those who do have come to accept what they can't change and then change what they can to redefine their lives.

In my case, I have shed the childhood quest to put back my family by creating a new one. I have shed the dream of never giving my children a divorce. I no longer picture the rocking chairs on the porch and the white picket fence. I am defining a new life with new goals and new adventures. In a very real sense, I am free of the limitations those dreams placed on me.

Anyone can move beyond the pain and suffering of any challenge. It just takes time and some very simple, but important processes designed for the specific problem. Kevin Pearce needed neurosurgeons and was lucky enough to have an incredible family.

We who are co-parenting with our abusers need specialists, too, to help us navigate this mostly unchartered terrain.

Unfortunately, there are not many professionals out there who are uniquely educated and skilled in the dynamics of domestic abuse and co-parenting because it is a very new phenomena. The 50/50 custody model has only become a legal standard in the last few years in many states around the country. In my state, the custody laws were changed in 2008. Florida no longer uses the terms "custody" and "visitation" and now use the terms "shared parenting" and "parenting time."

Meanwhile, our society still doesn't understand domestic abuse or how it plays out in custody disputes. One study conducted a decade ago examined the dynamics of domestic abuse post-divorce and its effects on child custody decisions. It began with the assumptions that mothers/victims had control over "granting" visitation to abusive fathers. This is not the case just 10 years later.

We, who co-parent today with our abusers, are the unfortunate trailblazers in this new world and will one day be case studies too. We victims understand innately that anyone who uses intimidation and exploitation should not be treated as an equal co-parent. The idea may be lofty and ideal, but in practice, doesn't work well and can be incredibly harmful.

However, we live in a time when professionals in the field are still learning and adequate training is rare.

It's hard to remain hopeful and happy when so many avenues are hopeless.

In my two-decade journey, married to an abuser and divorcing and co-parenting with one, I have seen almost a dozen therapists, gone through one domestic abuse advocacy center, at least five attorneys, two judges, one parenting coordinator and one mediator.

Those professionals who have helped me navigate this walk with an abuser have each given me something valuable to help me understand the playing field, whether positive or negative. Unfortunately, most did not show me that they understood the dynamics of the abuser/victim relationship, or better said, the power and control dynamics of domestic abuse.

When I found those who did, I was saved.

It is incredibly important to your recovery from abuse, and your walk co-parenting with an abuser, to work hard at finding the right professional. Your future happiness depends on it.

In my case, I found an incredible and unique social worker, who is passionate about helping those through the trauma that domestic abuse causes in women's lives. I was very lucky to be part of a pilot project at the local domestic abuse shelter in my town called Peaceful Paths. It was free, which was wonderful since I didn't have any money or insurance for therapy. I received two hours of therapy a week for about two years. My social worker, Jessica, was a gift from God and she helped me heal from the trauma of abuse. The pilot project has since changed and I am no longer a client through the program. I now have insurance that pays, so I still see Jessica as often as I can.

At some point in our sessions, Jessica diagnosed post traumatic stress disorder (PTSD) she said was from the trauma of domestic abuse. All the symptoms were there, sleepless nights, intrusive thoughts, hyper-sensitivity, and so on. I didn't realize that 10 years of living with someone who was repeatedly physically violent and the emotional abuse of an unfounded custody suit would cause PTSD, but once I learned more about it, it all made sense. Traumatic events cause emotional damage in all of us. Traumatic events are those shocks to our system that cause us to freeze in disbelief. The first time my ex tried to strangle me, it was a completely out of body experience. I could not compute this event. I would no more have expected him to walk into the room and disappear in a puff of smoke then what happened. I was in shock.

I didn't process that shock either. I buried it very quickly. I was pregnant and weeks from giving birth. My mother was coming to stay with us and help us manage our newborn. I was building the family that I had always wanted. Finding out that my husband was capable of something that could have killed both me and my baby was not something my mind could handle.

I went into denial almost immediately.

While he introduced violence into our marriage as a coping skills, I introduced denial and kept it for many, many years.

Jessica helped me unravel that and grieve for that young mother who lost her dream. Jessica also found that 9-year-old little girl inside of me, too, and helped her grieve for the family she lost as well.

It was powerful and got me to the next steps _ recovery from trauma and quieting PTSD. Emotional health gives me the strength I need when my abusive co-parent tries to engage with me again or I simply have to handle difficult relationships. Recovery from PTSD was so necessary for me to find my joy, be a better mother, daughter, friend and person.

I believe that the best first step for any survivor of domestic abuse is to get into the right kind of therapy as soon as possible.

I also believe you should interview your potential therapist, attorney, parent coordinator, mediator for the job. Remember, all these people are there because this is their business, their job and are first motivated by their own financial need. You want to find those special people who picked this profession because they are passionate about helping people like us and wanted to make it their life's work.

Jessica is one of those people. I know that money is not driving this women. She truly cares about people and their emotional health and she is passionate and educated about domestic abuse and how it is hurting our society and victims. She wants to see it stopped, as she knows that it can be.

My prayer is that you find someone like Jessica in your life. You will find your way out of this mess if you do. Most importantly, you and your children need emotional strength to manage this life you have with an abuser as a co-parent.

Until reform comes in the family court system, you may have no choice but to co-parent with someone who is not fit to compromise, be fair, empathize or share anything. This can cause trauma all over again. You need emotional support and healing. Good therapy can provide the medicine you need.

Here are my tips to find the right professional for this challenge:

Get Good Psychological Help

- I recommend a social worker (licensed clinical social worker or LCSW) over a psychologist. Social workers are trained differently. They will understand that you may be acting irrational, but it is because something irrational is happening to you. They don't start your therapy by asking you to fix yourself. I'm not suggesting that we all don't need that kind of analysis, but when someone is attacking you, you need to deal with that first. I never walked out of Jessica's office feeling worse than when I went in. Her therapy wasn't always easy, but it was incredibly helpful.
- You may be able to find a trained social worker at your local domestic abuse shelter or through your state domestic abuse hotline. I know that you are likely overwhelmed and maybe even suffering deeply at this point, but it is worth the effort to find the right person.

Once you have found a candidate for your therapy, here are the questions I would ask over the phone:

- Do you have experience with domestic abuse victims?
- Do you have experience with trauma treatment therapy?
- Have you received any training in working with domestic abuse victims?
- If yes, how much?
- Have you received any training in working with PTSD?
- How long does your trauma treatment therapy generally take?
- What else should I know about your work with domestic abuse?

The answers will help you figure out who your are dealing with. If he/she can't explain the domestic abuse training they received, then I would move on to another social worker. If you don't feel any empathy from the person as you are asking the questions, then this might not be the right fit. Don't be swayed by impressive credentials that are not relevant. I incorrectly hired a parenting coordinator because she told me that she had helped develop the co-parenting program with the local family court judge. However, I didn't realize at the time that she was investing in her model of success of helping "high-conflict" couples get along and work together. That was not going to help when co-parenting with an abuser. My attorney, who knew her, advised me to fire her when it was clear that she was only aggravating the problems.

Once again, I am thankful for the therapy I was receiving from Jessica, who helped me navigate the challenge this caused and gave me the emotional strength to be proactive.

More importantly, as the sometimes daily slings and arrows came at me from my abuser, Jessica was there to help me process the garbage so I could move on. I don't believe that any victim of domestic abuse forced to co-parent with their abuser can really recover from the trauma of abuse unless they are receiving excellent emotional support.

So many daily decisions are adversely affected by unstable emotions, especially when parenting. I am grateful that my therapist is there whenever I feel my emotional reactions are coming from that place in my heart born out of the trauma of abuse.

I know that I am a better parent because of her.

If you haven't found an excellent therapist yet, I recommend that above all else, you find one. You need this help because trying to heal from trauma alone is very difficult. Our society in general doesn't understand domestic abuse and you may be very hard pressed to find the support you need from the general populations. Family and friends struggle with understanding it. Family courts haven't connected the dots yet. Lawyers are not hired to sort out your feelings.

One family court judge told me that women will come into his courtroom assuming that the court is going to solve their emotional problems. That isn't going to happen, he said. Though I find that sentiment somewhat offensive on a number of levels, I understand that it is true; the courtroom is not the place for psychological growth.

It is also true that those who have been the victim of traumatic abuse don't need to solve emotional problems or "fix" themselves. As my therapist has told me time and again, they need to heal.

In my research, I have known victims who don't have time or money for therapy, who are really in pain. I often tell them that until they seek this emotional healing by an excellent professional, they are taking a risk that their decisions are clouded by the trauma of the abuse. In other words, you may be letting your abuser and the abuse enter too many parts of your life than is necessary.

These victims who are in the throes of post traumatic stress often look crazy to others and appear as though they are overreacting to life's challenges. This can lead to alienation and judgment from their family and friends.

But most importantly, without the proper healing received in trauma treatment therapy, you stand the risk of living life permanently handicapped by the open wounds of domestic abuse. You don't have to.

Of course, I am permanently scarred by the abuses by my ex-husband, but through therapy, my counselor has given me my sanity back and those scars are fading.

Step 3

Educate Yourself on the Dynamic of Abuse, the Law and Your Rights

No one would choose an abusive person hell-bent on gaining power and control in any circumstance as a parenting partner. Decision-making is part of daily life for parents and when there are decisions to be made, there are opportunities for those looking to win a battle.

When I was married to my abuser, there were days at a time when I handled all the decisions regarding our home-life. I would unconsciously select the dinner menu, what time the kids would go to bed, who did what chore, would we host a barbecue the coming weekend, and so on. My husband worked a lot and traveled for work a lot, and I was the stay-at-home mother manning the fort. But, there were times when my abuser seemed to need to dominate and without warning, he would suddenly care about some decision I made, no matter how insignificant, and begin to argue.

I could be in the middle of cooking a gourmet dinner for example, and he'd walk into the room survey what I was doing with a confused look on his face. Then, he would start barking his ideas as to how I should do it better. I love to cook and for me it's a very creative, introverted activity. I rarely use a recipe. I just bring together ingredients that come to me. I don't have to always be the cook, but when I do, I tune the world out and enjoy the experience. What I create is generally pretty good. I've worked as a chef several times in my life and had the fun of getting paid for my creations.

When my husband would decide to interject his "suggestions" it was nothing I sought or needed. I was in my element and he was intruding. But, if I didn't engage with him and accept his "help" then his suggestions would get more demanding and would escalate into a full-blown argument.

I always felt completely confused and baffled how something so insignificant would get out of hand so quickly. And suddenly the lovely dinner I was planning for my family was gone and our entire marriage and family life had just blown up by violence, hateful words or abandonment.

I would spend the next few days in a mess of emotions, blaming myself for letting a simple argument get so out of control. Why didn't I just do what he asked, then I would not have been hit or left?

I lived life like that for more than a decade. After I divorced my abuser, I still found myself in his line of sight from time to time when he seemed ready for a fight. My locked front door of my own home stayed between us more times than once when I feared his violence. I was grateful.

But, during all of those years, I truly believed that I was part of the dynamic that caused his outbursts, anger and violence. Of course he blamed me repeatedly for it, but I blamed myself, too. I assumed that he was right about me, that I was stubborn and had high expectations. I assumed that I was wrong to have desires and needs that I was willing to achieve. I thought that made me wrong. Even when that therapist explained to me that my choices were to leave my husband or be his doormat, I still believed that choosing my life somehow made me wrong.

It wasn't until years later that I learned something new: I wasn't wrong to have my own ideas, wants and desires, or wrong to put effort into achieving them.

Through education, some of it accidental, I changed a lot of my thinking about domestic abuse and the trauma it causes. But, I also learned a lot about myself, society and the current state of the fight to end domestic violence.

My education began first as a way to seek validation about the turmoil in my life. I opened a blog about my daily experience as a single mother with an abusive ex-husband. The blog was excellent therapy. I wrote in real time about my experiences and feelings. I called it bruisedwoman.com. I didn't have much of a following, but that didn't matter. For me, it was pure therapy.

As I moved through the journey of abuse and healing, I became more interested in the journey of others and I why domestic abuse was so hard to stop. My curiosity is part of who I am. Before I had children and became a stay-at-home mother, I was a newspaper journalist and I was trained how to research just about any topic, quickly.

I began to study more and more America's current epidemic of domestic abuse.

As I did, I began to realize that I was a textbook domestic abuse victim, and I began to want to know why and what causes some men to hit. So, thanks to Google and Kindle, I had access to more material than I could ever need to learn about abuse, narcissism and the statistics and stories all over the country. I also began to read the laws.

Through this process, I found out that though I couldn't stop most of my ex's abusive behavior toward me, some abusive behaviors after divorce aren't legal.

I learned about the federal Violence Against Women Act that doesn't allow domestic abuser to harass their victims, even after the end of the relationship. This law acknowledges that intimate partner abusers will always be that to the victim, no matter the end of the relationship, and abusers don't have the right to continue to try to harass their victims.

I learned that in my state, Florida, domestic abuse victims are not forced to use a parenting coordinator with their abusive co-parents and can opt out at any time if the coordinator is just giving the abuser a power and control playing field.

I also learned about the psychology of abuse and the effects of post traumatic stress disorder, or PTSD. My therapist had diagnosed me with the disorder and I learned a lot about how it was effecting me. It was a relief to learn, for example, that waking in the middle of the night because my mind wouldn't shut off replaying the abuse over and over was a symptoms of PTSD. I wasn't crazy, I was suffering from a trauma in my life. Our brains naturally try to reset the events to eliminate the trauma, I learned.

PTSD is defined by the Nebraska Department of Veteran's Affairs as:

PTSD, or Post traumatic Stress Disorder, is a psychiatric disorder that can occur following the experience or witnessing of a life-threatening events such as military combat, natural disasters, terrorist incidents, serious accidents, or physical or sexual assault in adult or childhood. Most survivors of trauma return to normal given a little time. However, some people will have stress reactions that do not go away on their own, or may even get worse over time. These individuals may develop PTSD. People who suffer from PTSD often relive the experience through nightmares and flashbacks, have difficulty sleeping, and feel detached or estranged, and these symptoms can be severe enough and last long enough to significantly impair the person's daily life.
http://www.ptsd.ne.gov/what-is-ptsd.html

The Department also reports about 8 percent of Americans have suffered from PTSD and the most common cause of the disorder for women is: rape, sexual molestation, physical attack, being threatened with a weapon, and childhood physical abuse.

I also found out that there is an entire community of survivors of domestic abuse and I started to connect with them through social media, my blog and around my community.

I interviewed victims, too, like the wife of a former NFL football player. Dewan Smith-Williams came out as a victim after Baltimore Ravens player Ray Rice hit his wife in an elevator and it was caught on security video.

I interviewed therapists, judges, lawyers and victims. I started a support group for local victims and brought in speakers on the subject of domestic abuse and legal experts who work to help victims file restraining orders and collect child support.

Eventually, I created a survey of victims and began collecting data about abuse after divorce and how it affected child custody cases and co-parenting.

I continue to research the subject today because information for me as always helped me get my head around the simple fact that abusers make the choice to abuse and it doesn't matter what you do, or say. Once you have one in your life, your life will never be the same.

Before I educated myself on this dynamic, I was constantly shocked by what was happening. I would be shocked each time my husband attacked me. I was shocked each time I felt society let me down. I was shocked whenever a family member or friend didn't quite understand or continued to pretend that my abuser wasn't one.

As my therapist taught me, shock can be another way of describing trauma. Trauma she said is what happens when your emotions are frozen after the event, like when you gasp at the sight of something horrible, but don't exhale. Your brain shuts it out and you don't feel the sadness over what happened. Of course, when my husband hit me, I was deeply sad because it meant that he was not healthy enough to be in an intimate relationship. But instead of sitting on the floor in a puddle of tears that should have come the first time he tried to strangle me and ended my hope of a normal family and healthy union, I froze that feeling and tried to get my fantasy back.

Years and years of that created deep, trauma that never healed. It was a break in my body that was never set right and grew worse over time.

Living with untreated PTSD means that every day relationships can be a challenge. Victims can remain hyper-sensitive to any affront afraid that it is a signal of impending abuse.

Educating myself about all of this, and good trauma treatment therapy helped me heal and dial down the symptoms of PTSD.

Learning about the laws that applied to my case with my ex as we co-parented our children also helped me know when I needed to react to his threats and when I could ignore him and move on. Educating myself about the law took care of a lot of fear.

My ex often threatened when I did not agree to his desire that he would take us back to court. If he wanted a change to the schedule or thought I was not following the court-ordered parenting plan, then I would find a nasty email making the threat.

I have hundreds and hundreds of emails from my abuser that accuse me of all sorts of unfounded offenses and assigned motives that were far from reality.

Co-parenting, at least the way that I was doing it, gave my abuser, the man I divorced because I found him unsafe, the right to force communication and opportunity to abuse me further.

I had to find another way. This constant contact was going to kill me.

So, I started to research co-parenting and why it came into favor in family courts. I learned that co-parenting had quickly become the standard in family courts around the country just a few years ago because it made child custody cases a lot quicker and easier to handle. And this standard has been formed without much academic evidence that it really is best for children. Instead, it seemed to be based in the parents' rights to act as parents. Of the studies and papers I could find in favor of co-parenting, all reported that co-parenting works best post divorce when both parents agree and can rise above their own personal needs and compromise with their co-parenting partner in healthy ways.

However, all the studies also reported that when domestic abuse is part of the relationship, co-parenting is not recommended because it continues to give the abuser a path to gain power and control while exploiting the victims and children. Only if the abuser has acknowledges his responsibility in the abuse and agrees to stop the power and control activities going forward, should co-parenting be applied.

Well, it was clear that those who study the dynamic of these relationships don't believe in co-parenting when there is a history of family abuse, but family court practices aren't getting that information.

I learned too that many experts are working on educating judges about this dynamic.

However, my family couldn't wait for these changes to come. We had to find a better way. That is when I read about parallel parenting, a method used when cooperation is not possible and courts award a version of joint custody.

Parallel parenting isn't easy but for me, it allowed me to disconnect from my abuser and focus instead on parenting. There are also conditions that need to be in place in order for this to bring comfort and peace to the domestic abuse victim and her concern about her children's safety. Parallel parenting also is a way to institute the "No Contact" rule advised when a victim is trying to break the emotional chains connected to a narcissistic abuser.

If you are considering parallel parenting, I recommend that you read as much as you can about it first to make sure it is right for your family. I've written about it in more depth here: *http://divorcedmoms.com/blogs/thriving-in-crazy-land/coparenting-vs-parallel-parenting-whats-the-difference/*

Step 3 of my journey, getting educated, has saved me many times throughout this journey and has helped me help others, protect my children and myself, get treated for PTSD, stop living daily life with my abuser in my head, and on and on. Education for me has given me back my life.

Most importantly, education on this matter has helped me understand domestic abuse and why it happened to me and to some extend, forgive my abuser. I don't let him off the hook or pretend anymore that he is not an abuser. I will never forget the feeling of his hands around my throat or trying to rise after a beating or the threat of losing custody of my children. But, I don't believe that he truly understands what he is doing. Nor do I believe that he is out to get me. I believe that he is broken emotionally and hurt deeply and has no way of handling that well.

He suffers, too, and in the end, I do pity him. It is not likely that my abuser will ever really love someone or feel someone loving him. His relationship with his children will never rise to a high level. He isn't likely to rise to the level he sees himself. And his behavior more often then not drives people away. I have witnessed him being ridiculed and scorned for years. And in all these years, I don't think he really has but one true friend.

He may believe that he is powerful, charming and in total control of his life, but the facts of his life show a different story.

In the end, I pity him and feel sorry for my children, who must live the rest of their lives knowing that their father beat their mother and then sued her for their custody.

How can I feel anything other than sad about that.

Step 4

Find the right Legal Representation

If you are co-parenting with your abuser or about to, it is very important that you understand the laws in your state, the federal laws that deal with violence against women and the way those laws are enforced in your community.

Not all jurisdictions are alike and not all laws are enforced. The law, a family court order, an excellent attorney, these can be the tools that can help you set boundaries in your life to hold back abuse.

There is a lot to consider and understand when it comes to the law and the role it plays in co-parenting.

Knowing that you are getting the best advice and help from the right legal representative is critical.

Excellent therapy helps get you emotionally strong for the days and years ahead. Excellent legal advice give you the strategies you need to mitigate your abusers attacks.

It is not enough to use an attorney with a reputation of being a "bull-dog" or a real fighter. I believe you need an attorney who understands the dynamic of abuse and how that plays out in the long haul. If you live in a small community, you may not be able to find one. Maybe you can find one who is willing to learn about it.

http://www.leadershipcouncil.org/docs/ABA_custody_myths.pdf or
http://www.leadershipcouncil.org/1/pas/dv.html are two very excellent resources to share with your attorney.

You also don't want an attorney who paints you as a co-conspirator in a high-conflict divorce. You are not, and that label rarely helps a victims of domestic abuse.

You want an attorney who is willing to do the work necessary to show that you are the victim of domestic abuse and that your abuser hasn't stopped his quest for power and control. Also, your attorney should be trying to enlist the court's help in protecting you and your children from further abuse.

My advice to any victim of abuse is to accept that your abuser may very well get shared parenting time, so don't go in arguing and enraged over it. You will look uncooperative and crazy and fulfill their label of co-conspirator.

But, don't hesitate to state your fears about the future and the challenges you and your children have already faced because your ex is your abuser.

I also benefited from a very detailed parenting plan after my ex-husband unsuccessfully sued me for custody five years after our divorce. A multi-page court order that instructed each of us what to do going forward was the only good that came out of this frivolously action. I knew when I signed it that I could live with and follow what we had set down. It took eight months of mediation, motion hearings and lawyer conference calls, but it got worked out.

I had an excellent attorney who didn't hesitate to introduce into the process very quickly that my ex was an admitted abuser, something that I did not introduce in our original divorce. I believe that, had she not done that, my life would be very different today. There are many attorneys out there who don't want victims to bring up the abuse in family court because they know that many judges will assume it is a ploy to tarnish the other parent.

My attorney told me that it would not be easy to introduce abuse five years after the last physical incident. But, she never argued with me about it and listened to me tell my story.

She introduced it in the very first motion hearing and my ex immediately said to his attorney, "But I didn't hit the kids."

From then on, domestic abuse was part of the discussion and when I was deposed by his attorney, the first question he asked was to describe in details the incidents of physical abuse. I put on record the years of physical violence and when it was my ex's turn to answer questions, my attorney got him to admit to it all, right there in front of his two attorneys and the court stenographer.

That afternoon, after months and months of his dominating threats, he settled. I don't know exactly why, because I have learned not to trust the words of an abuser, but I do imagine that his attorneys advised him to do so after hearing the only real evidence presented, five hours of our testimony.

Despite this "victory" in the offices that day, the next few weeks of finishing up the parenting plan and details, my abuser began to hit hard again. My attorney was by me every step of the way, helping me understand what could and couldn't happen. She has been there again many times through the years after the custody suit to help me when my ex has made threats, unfounded accusations and demands.

I was lucky to have found her and I was even more fortunate that my ex-husband was ordered to pay her fees. Tens of thousands were spent through that process and I am thankful, not by me.

Most victims are not that fortunate.

I know many women whose bank accounts have been drained by legal fees and costs and they have nothing to show for it but more pain.

Our system fails us all when abusers are allowed to use the judicial system to further abuse. I have often wondered why judges are so willing to let abusers drag their victims back to court so many times using children as pawns in the process.

But, I remind myself that this dynamic of domestic abuse and co-parenting is just so new in our society that family courts just haven't caught up. After all, when my parents divorced, there was no question that we would live full-time with my mother. We spent many weekends with my dad, but my mother had full custody.

No court ordered my parents to cooperate or spend families celebrations together or force contact between the two. They were divorced and they never had to speak to each other again.

Further, our judicial system is overrun with cases and dockets are packed. Judges are overworked, under appreciated and often under trained to handle everything that is on their plate.

One family court judge I interviewed on this subject told me that women who come into the family court room looking for justice for the wrongs of the marriage are going to be disappointed. They are not there to settle the score, he said. They are gathered there to figure out a plan to go forward while being fair to both parties and really aren't there to discuss what is best for the children. Most cases take less than an hour or two to adjudicate. I believe our children's future deserve more than that.

Domestic abuse is still widely marginalized in our society. Recent media attention has moved the cause forward, but in the end most people don't want to discuss it, are biased or consider the topic dirty laundry best left to the couple.

Those who are not abused or haven't studied abuse, really don't understand it because they don't have a frame of reference. Why would anyone beat or knowingly exploit someone they love? This question leads to those questions we have all heard or even said ourselves: If it were so bad, why would she stay? What did she do to cause him to get so mad? These questions put the responsibility on the victim and so it's no wonder our justice system does too.

An excellent attorney, coupled with an excellent therapist, can help you process not only the abuse you faced, but also the unintentional abuses of society.

If you are just beginning to look for an attorney or have decided to change your current representation, I recommend that you call your local domestic abuse center first and ask for a referral.

If there is no center in your town, then I recommend calling your state hotline.

Getting a referral is far better than Googling attorneys in your area and picking one that makes the list. Be cautious about attorneys who say they are domestic abuse attorney. Most mean that they help abusers handle a criminal charge.

Once you get a few names, try to get a free meeting. Even if you don't think you have any money for legal representation, set up a few free consultations. Most attorneys will do this. And they will also assess if you will be able to collect attorney's fees from your abuser. In my case, my attorney never asked me for a dime and agreed to take the case because in my state she was confident that she could get fees awarded. She was right. But I know many women who weren't so fortunate.

I also signed up for a **pre-paid legal service** for about $30 a month. In the early days of our new parenting plan, I often called this hotline and spoke directly with an attorney in my state to discuss what rights I had to move in one direction or another. I kept this service for a several years and I was very glad that I did. I never got the same attorney on the phone, but they had my court documents and parenting plan on file and they would tell me the law and how it applied.

One particular event happened when my ex wanted to make a change to the plan, and when I didn't want to do it, he got our parenting coordinator involved. He did this often whenever he wanted me to do as he wished. He told her that because I wouldn't make the change, I was showing I wasn't cooperative and she agreed. This lack of cooperation, would be used against me in court and could jeopardize my custody, he claimed.

I was shocked yet again and could not understand why our coordinator would suggest that though we had spent months and months hammering out a detailed parenting plan with lawyers, a judge and a mediator, I would be in the wrong for not agreeing to a change.

After fretting and worrying about my children's custody, I got myself together and reached for the phone and called my pre-paid legal hotline service.

I told the attorney on-call the story and he told me clearly and emphatically that I would not be judged harshly by a judge for following his court order. He said that no matter what the coordinator said, I was not obligated to agree to anything different than the parenting plan.

I was so relieved, but this coordinator was so confident in her guidance to us, I couldn't understand, I told the attorney. He repeated again that the law was the law and the order was the order and I didn't have to make a single change.

"Are you sure?" I asked one more time.

"Yes," he said. And then he added that **parenting coordinators are not lawyers or judges and may not understand the law**. He then went on to tell me that in my state parenting coordinators could not testify in favor of one parent over another in subsequent motions and could not provide family counseling or even counsel the children.

I was shocked again because our parenting coordinator had done all of that.

Over the course of several months, I began to share what I was learning from my pre-paid legal service attorneys and the few consultations with my custody suit attorney with the coordinator. I let her know that she didn't seem to acknowledge the dynamic of abuse or the current order's directives. I even gave her a letter from my therapist and the head of the local domestic abuse center left several messages for her in an attempt to educate this woman.

She was polite but unresponsive.

Finally, my legal advisors told me it was time to fire her, something I didn't realize until I did this research that I could do. As it turned out, any domestic abuse victim in my state can refuse to use a parenting coordinator if that process is aggravating the dynamic.

My abuser was not happy about it, as expected, and I have several distasteful emails from him that show it. But, I was confident because my legal help was confident and it was an excellent decision. Years have past since and I am no longer re-traumatized by the ignorance inbred in the system.

Here are the key questions I would ask a prospective attorney:
- Do you provide an initial free consultation?
- Have you worked with domestic abuse victims in family court before?
- Do you know which judges are best to handle family court issues when there is a history of domestic violence?
- Do you specialize in divorce and child custody?
- Have you received any training in domestic abuse or personality disorders, such as narcissism?
- Can you help me get _____ (fill in the blank for what you hope will happen, such as full physical custody or a detailed parenting plan, etc.)
- Who do you think will have to pay attorney's fees?
- How long and how much money will this take?

If an attorney tells you that introducing domestic abuse into a divorce or child custody hearing is not wise, I urge you to hang up and make the next call. Don't get me wrong, it is not easy to introduce domestic abuse into family court. Judges, and lawyers, assume you are making it up in order to get an edge up in the battle. If they believe you, and they may if you can explain what happened without reacting to the trauma the disbelief causes, they may say that it doesn't matter in the eyes of the law. But, it is a very important part of the story and you need to report it.

Strangers in your life, like your new attorney or the judge, don't know if you are telling the truth or how domestic abuse infects your daily life. They need to learn this about you and just like any relationship, getting to know you takes time. Give your legal team that time and don't resent them for it. If you show resentment, which is normal, then they could very well chalk it up to your problem and play right into the hand of your abuser. Abusers often come across as the normal, calm parent in family court and paint you as the crazy one.

You can't stop your abuser for what he may say, but you can control what you do and say. Don't allow your actions to be directed by his. Instead, try to understand that your legal team starts from an assumption that justice is blind, that both parents are deserving and that people lie, even their clients. Believe it or not, they are not there to determine what is best for your individual children and evaluate your unique family. I know that makes no sense, but it is true. They are there to win their case and use the law and the judge to their advantage. Your abuser's attorney can be extremely nasty toward you and no one will stop him as long as he follows the rules of the courtroom.

Be patient and as calm as you can be, then be factual. Let them know the details of what happened or is happening. Our abusers spend a lot of time trying to make us take responsibility for their actions. Too often it builds in us a very quick defensive response. Strangers, and even friends, don't understand why we are so defensive and it doesn't work in our favor. Many women have lost their custody because they reacted emotionally and understandable to cross examination by their abuser's attorney. You should be aware that his attorney is going to try to push your buttons to get a heated reaction out of you. If you are in that position, disconnect your feelings from the attack and remember it's all a ploy to get you to react. Don't.

Your legal advisors can help if you pick the right people and don't expect more than they are there to do. Know that family court is not the place where your abuser is finally going to get what he deserves. Our system doesn't work that way.

Instead, focus on what you think your children need the most. Focus on the issues and not how he is acting or communicating or anything else for that matter. Think about what is best for your kids, then communicate that to your attorney.

In my case, I didn't want my kids to move back and forth every few days between their parents' home or lose custody all together. I knew this demand by my ex would really hurt our kids. I never once considered giving in on this point. I held firm because I decided that though a judge might make this decision, I was not going to. As a result, after the suit, my kids woke up in their beds in my house every school day morning. They rarely had to worry about where their school projects were or phone chargers or any of the other things that kids carry today.

You might also consider going through the legal system without an attorney. I know some women who have done this. They make this choice mostly because they have run out of money. I do think this should be used as a last resort and with lots of thought and understanding. Every situation is different. I have represented myself in court before and found that the judge actually took extra time to help me understand what was happening. I've heard others have had similar experiences. But, it's risky and should be done with extreme caution. Studies have shown that women without council don't fair as well in family court as those who have an attorney.

Domestic abuse victims' advocate, researcher and author Lundy Bancroft recommends in his book *"When Dad Hurts Mom. Helping Your Children Heal the Wounds of Witnessing Abuse"* that it is best to you hire an excellent, qualified attorney who understands this unique dynamic and will work hard for you. Only if you can't find this type of attorney, does he recommend representing yourself. He writes in his book that hiring a bad attorney to represent you in court can truly hurt you and your children and cost you a lot of money, so don't do that. *(THE BERKLEY PUBLISHING GROUP Published by the Penguin Group, Bancroft, Lundy (2005-03-01). When Dad Hurts Mom: Helping Your Children Heal the Wounds of Witnessing Abuse . Penguin Publishing Group. Kindle Edition.)*

In the end, your abuser and the legal system will focus almost all of their energy and attention on you and your ex, not the children.

You must not let your focus follow. You must evaluate each step in the process through the lens of reality: Your co-parent is your abuser and your children need at least one sane parent.

Step 5

Document Everything and Tell Friends and Family

If you are about to begin to co-parent with your abuser or fear that the court will order you to, then it is very important that you keep detailed records for future actions you may face in court.

You also need to share the truth about your union and post-divorce experience with others in your circle, your friends, family, school officials, co-workers, etc.

I know that this goes against a lot of what you believe or how you lived when you were with your abuser. Most victims hide the abuse they suffered in their marriage and incorrectly take responsibility for it. This causes shame. Our shame is part of the reason domestic abuse continues because we want to hide it as much as our abusers want us to.

But, sharing your story with others, especially people valued by your ex, can help stop it. Even if it doesn't, your "testimony" to others is documentation.

Documentation is evidence and evidence is the only thing admissible in court. Judges look for patterns when trying to understand the dynamics of a divorcing couple. If you have documented the events that prove your ex is abusive and can show a pattern of coercive behavior, you have a better chance of getting the attention of the court.

The National Domestic Violence Hotline recommends the following ways to document abuse for court:
- Verbal testimony from you or your witnesses
- Medical reports of injuries
- Dated pictures of any injuries
- Police reports of when you or a witness called the police
- Household objects torn or broken by the abuser
- Pictures of your household in disarray after a violent episode
- Pictures of weapons used by the abuser against you
- A personal diary or calendar in which you documented the abuse as it happened

http://www.thehotline.org/2014/05/building-your-case-how-to-document-abuse/

If you have been the victim of physical abuse, then I know that the last thing you are thinking about after getting beat up, is to take a selfie, but a picture is worth a thousands words.

Maybe you saw the horrifying pictures of NFL football player Greg Hardy's girlfriend's bruised body. Those pictures, like the video of NFL player Ray Rice knocking out his wife in an elevator, caused an enormous uproar in our society.

If you are more the victim of financial, emotional or psychological abuse, then you have other documents to collect.

When my ex sued me for custody long after our divorce, I walked into the first meeting with my attorney with five years of daily calendars, in hardcopy. I had marked each time my ex-husband canceled his scheduled, weekly visitation. In five years, he had canceled about 25 times a year and I had a written record of proof. I marked why he canceled, or at least the reason he told me. Most of the time, he said he was traveling for work. Sometimes, he canceled to go on vacation or for reasons he didn't share. I had the children at my home whenever he canceled, which was fine with me. Frankly, I saw it as a blessing and didn't give him a hard time about so many cancelations.

A few times and more often as the kids got older and had their own social, school and sports schedules, I would cancel his visitation because my children couldn't make it. I had full custody of the children and was in charge of their schedules.

Maybe twice in five years, I changed our schedule of weekly visitations because of my own needs.

I had all of this written down, day after day, year after year, for five years. So, when my ex made the claim that I was keeping him from the kids, I had proof that I was not.

I don't know why I kept meticulous track. Even as technology moved us all to electronic calendars, I keep an old-fashion daybook in pen. My attorney let me know this was the best thing I could have done. This was difficult-to-dispute evidence to contradict his claim that I was keeping the kids from seeing their dad.

Because my ex was a sportswriter covering the NFL, his work was publicly documented in articles online for anyone to see and each of his articles began with the name of the city he was visiting. This gave my attorney third-party proof of his travel schedule to support my day-planner.

The evidence showed my ex would have a difficult time maintaining custody of our children with so much of his time on the road.

I also kept every email he ever sent me. I printed them each out and put them in a binder. It was three inches thick. I tried to categorize them in a order with meaning for my attorney.

During our marriage, my ex would sometimes write me handwritten letters of apologies for the abuses and once wrote me a letter that if we were to divorce, I was the better parent and should have full custody of our kids.

I kept each one and handed them to my attorney during his custody suit against me.

I also turned over my phone records that showed how often I called him each month to give him updates on the kids. It also showed how often he called me, dozens of times a month.

Though the content of the calls were not recorded by me, the simple volume of calls made it difficult for him to prove that I was not communicating with him in parenting issues.

When my ex-husband's attorney was deposing me, he asked me how I was so sure of canceled visitation or the details of an alleged email, I said calmly, "Because I have the records."

He looked up at me and said, "You have calendars and copies of the emails for the last five years?" he asked in disbelief. "Yes," I said.

He shot his gaze at my attorney about to say something when my attorney cut him off and said, "Oh, we will be providing you with copies."

He had only one questions about the documents after that:

"Why did you keep five years of emails and daily planners?" he asked with a tone in his voice as if this was strange.

"I don't know, I guess I figured one day I would need them," I said.

That ended that line of questioning.

Documentation is very important and you should make it a practice to keep it as long as you are co-parenting with your abuser. Don't pick through those records and edit out those emails that embarrass you. Remember that as a victim of an abusive union, you are not to blame or the cause of abuse. No matter what. But, that doesn't mean that you haven't fired off a nasty email to your abuser or have done or said something that you regret. Don't hide those emails from your attorney and don't pretend that his abusive behavior hasn't brought out the worst in you. This is understandable.

When I told my attorney that sometimes I wasn't the nicest ex-wife, my attorney looked at me and said, "So. That makes you normal."

Always be honest with your attorney.

Don't let the fear of documentation prevent you from keeping it or producing it. It is very important.

Here are some examples of what you may want to keep:
- A handwritten, dated diary of any unfair treatment you have experienced
- A handwritten day planner of visitations, missed events, etc.
- Phone records
- A list of school activities, teacher conferences, etc., with dates, times and who was there
- Screenshots of text messages from your ex
- Late payments of child support or medical bills
- Evidence of travel
- Evidence of cyberstalking on social media
- Any handwritten letters from him or from loved ones about him
- Pictures of your family before and after divorce
- Written comments from teachers and psychologists about your children

This list can be as long as you want. The point is to keep a written record of all your interactions for as long you feel that he is a legal threat to you.

Without it, and you may find yourself in a true he-said/she-said and your only evidence is your testimony and his. This leaves everything up to the judge to determine who he likes, believes, and sides with. Most abusers are very good at winning over people in such circumstances.

Share the truth about the abuse with other people in your children's lives. If you don't, those around you and your children will not have the correct context of your actions and may not understand you.

If you think that your children are in danger _ and frankly I don't know of a single parent who sends their children off to spend time alone with their abuser who doesn't _ then you will need other people to be aware of what is possible.

When I began telling people about the abuse, I was embarrassed and it was hard. Today, after letting everyone know about the abuse I suffered, I share it without emotion.

Here is what I tell my employers:

"I am a survivor of domestic abuse. I have sought treatment and tried to address the scars as best I can, but sometimes there are side effects that creep into my daily life. I have support to deal with it when it does. I don't expect this to happen, but if my abuser comes to my place of work, please know that he is not welcome and I may be in danger, so please act accordingly."

Here is what I tell school counselors, teachers, coaches, pediatricians:

"My child comes from a home where there was chronic domestic abuse by the hand of my ex-husband. We now co-parent, which makes for a difficult dynamic that is a unique challenge for my child. My ex and I are not friends and don't always work well together, so I ask for your help by sharing information about our child separately and understanding if things don't always make sense. Also, if you see anything that causes you concern for our child, please let me know. I appreciate your willingness to help our child. Thank you."

Here is what I have told friends and family:

"I have something to tell you that I have kept from you all these years. During my marriage, I was physically and emotionally abused and that is the reason I sought a divorce. It has been a long and difficult journey that has included a diagnosis of PTSD. As a result, I have as little contact with my ex as possible and I would appreciate it if you could refrain from talking about him to me or speak about me to him. I am sorry if this is too much information or makes you uncomfortable, but it is very necessary for my healing and future safety that I set these boundaries."

I have told various versions of all of those quotes above when I have felt that it was appropriate to give a friend perspective or enlist the help of people during a particular incident. I also let my ex know that I have done so because I found that the only thing that seems to stop domestic abuse is the public awareness of it, both broadly and within my own circumstance.

I once asked our friends, family and even strangers to sign a petition that I shared with my ex calling for civility when co-parenting our children.

Abuse in my circumstance is no longer something I keep quietly behind closed doors. I am a public advocate and a vocal supporter of the cause to end it.

Letting people know about abuse is not an act of revenge, as victims know. Its an act of survival as we navigate through this journey.

Step 6

Respond Only When It's Necessary, Do Not Respond When It's Not

Victims of abuse have a difficult, long walk to recovery in every way. The trauma of abuse by the person who is supposed to love you the most is life altering. Throw in shared children and the current court climate of cooperative parenting, and victims have an uphill journey to get back to a normal life and emotional stability.

Your abuser, unless he has been through a lot of therapy and has shown you a long pattern of respect and understanding, probably doesn't care about your bruised and battered walk. In fact, to many abusers, narcissists in particular, your pain and suffering makes them feel powerful and in charge. The more vulnerable you are, the more attractive you are to use as a pawn in an abuser's need to dominate others.

I think of it this way: An abuser can be like a vortex in the middle of the lake, sucking in everything that comes its way. The vortex doesn't care if it sucks in a fish, a leaf or a boat full of people. It just continues to spin around and around taking in everything in its path.

An abuser, I believe, may not really care who he dominates on any given day, just that he has had the rush of the feeling as often as possible. Some even believe they are addicted to it.

When you get near your abuser, either figuratively or literally, you are in danger of getting sucked into his vortex. If you are feeling weak that day or he sees you as vulnerable, then you become easy picking.

It took me a long time to understand this and I often assumed that the exchanges between my ex and myself blew up or spiraled out of control because of a miscommunications or misunderstanding. I would replay the event over and over in my head trying to understand just what happened that led to such a mess.

When my husband first put his hands on me so many years ago, I couldn't believe it. In the years that followed, I could never understand why he did that and introduced violence into our marriage. I was sitting in a rocking chair, *nine months pregnant*, no threat to anyone, no reason for him to charge and begin to squeeze my neck.

It made no sense to me.

When I began to research domestic abuse, I read in many places that statistically, abusers introduced physical violence into the relationship first when their partners are pregnant. Ok, our situation fit the norm. I still couldn't understand why. I didn't understand why he attacked me, a big, exhausted pregnant woman with no ability to hurt him.

Finally, it clicked in my therapist's office. He attacked me that day because I wasn't a threat to him. I was an easy target in order to get that rush of dominance he sought. I didn't know that abusers are always trying to dominate others in order to feel good about themselves. It doesn't mean that in every relationship they are dominating. Sometimes they look for sympathy instead or find the rush in being the "go-to" guy who people admire. Dominating others brings abusers pleasure. It fulfills for them a basic need.

Abusers often see people differently than you and I. Abusers see people as things. And they pay attention to how those things make them feel. The psychology is deep and multi-layered but in the end, abusers are unpredictable and dangerous. It is best to stay away.

We can't fix them or say the right thing that will bring out the best in them. Oh, maybe for a minute, but it can take lots of exhausting and dangerous effort to achieve even the slightest glimpse of kindness from an abuser when he wants to be dominating.

However, if you disconnect from an abuser and he doesn't want you to, that evil, hurtful man in your life, can become a saint right before your eyes. Abusers can't stand to lose an object that they can control, so they can use faux kindness to bring you back in. Beware, it is not likely to continue and abusers can just as quickly flip their behaviors to dominating jerks all over again.

There is so much information out there about narcissists and the mindset of a domestic abuser. As I said earlier, it is in your best interest to learn as much as you can about the dynamics of this type of person. I don't recommend ever trusting your abuser again, no matter what he is offering.

Instead, it is best for your own recovery to set the goal of "No Contact." This is the term used to describe the strategy used to get a narcissist out of your life and give you a chance to heal. http://www.goodtherapy.org/blog/no-contact-rule-recovering-from-narcissistic-abuse-0618136

No Contact mean absolutely no contact of any kind. No emails, phone calls, social media posts or shares, no messages, no acknowledgment of him at all. Not even eye contact when you are in the same room together.

Experts say that No Contact gives the victim the best chance of healing and if maintained by the victim for a certain length of time, the abusers will eventually stop seeking the emotional high from dominating you and move on, unfortunately to other people.

Psychologists advise that when dealing with an abusive narcissist, there are only two choices: 1. Stay engaged and put yourself in harms way or 2. Stay away from him for good.

No Contact is not easy to pull off when you share children together, especially young children. As a victim of abuse, you know when the court awards unsupervised time to your abuser, you are often anxious about the time your children now have alone with the person who was willing to abuse you. Maintaining contact gives you the ability to react if anything goes wrong.

You may also have a small amount of influence over his actions with the children if you maintain a connection, however fragile and difficult. For years, I was able to do that. I felt more secure pretending to be friends with my ex than actually showing him how much I disliked him. That faux friendship enable me to be there for my kids if anything went wrong and they needed help.

Too often mothers are painted as overbearing and unwilling to let well-intended dads take care of their children. That may be true in some cases, but victims of domestic abuse know all too well that life with an abuser can be truly dangerous.

I wasn't hovering around my children when they were with their dad. By staying friendly with him, I was informed of things in real time and could react to things as needed. One time, while my young son was with his dad, he called me at the end of the day to tell me about school. He told me that he didn't feel well and had a headache. I asked him why and he told me that he fell off the merry-go-round at school and hit his head. He told me how he had to sit out the rest of recess and felt like he was going to throw up.

I asked him to put his father on the phone and then told my ex that he needed to take our son to the hospital because these were symptoms of a concussion. My ex told me he knew about the fall and wasn't worried and I was making too much about it. I was surprised by this reactions because as a sportswriter covering the NFL, my ex knew the dangers of concussions. But, he would not be swayed to act. So, I called the kids' pediatrician and set up a conference call with my ex. After going down a checklist with us, the medical professional told us our son need to go to the ER right away.

My ex was still hesitating. So, I said while still on the conference call, that I could drive over to take our son to the hospital and the doctor said that would be a good idea. I asked my ex if he planned to come to the ER too or stay home. He said he would follow us in his car. After the CAT scan, the doctor instructed us that our son had to be awakened every few hours and my ex agreed to let me take him home in order to keep watch.

I didn't understand at the time why my ex was so insistent that it was no big deal. Maybe he had other plans that night that he didn't want to interrupt with a trip to the ER. Maybe he was embarrassed that he hadn't called the doctor himself. Maybe making me look hyperbolic to the children made him feel good. But, using our child's health in this way wasn't acceptable and I am glad that our "friendship" enabled me to get our child the medical attention he needed.

However, staying connected to an abuser comes with great costs. First, it is exhausting because abusers don't make a lot of sense, are unpredictable, scary and often point fingers when it's time to take responsibility. In the worst case, they can cause their victims real physical, emotional and financial damage.

As my children have grown into adults, I have transitioned to the "No Contact" approach and feel that it has been a benefit to my emotional health. I have also come to understand that my children are learning from this as well. Of course, it sucks that they don't have me to rush them to the hospital if they hit their heads, but they are also learning what to do for themselves. They are learning how to manage their own relationships with their parents. These are important lessons for any child, but maybe more so for children of abusers.

No matter what anyone tells you, abuser abuse because they want to and they can. People don't cause other people to abuse. They are not emotionally healthy. They may never hit their children, though the majority of them do, but they can emotionally hurt their children in many ways. Children will never truly be protected from the pain of having an abuser for a parent.

We can only help them process it and learn to live with it in much the same ways we do.

My children see me set my boundaries and in every relationship, a certain degree of respect is required or I am moving on and shutting down the relationship. In other words, they see that there are consequences for abuse. I am hoping that they will never see abuse as acceptable and will never tolerate it.

No Contact gives me the space I need to heal from those slings and arrows he throws that get through and touch my heart.

I have set up artificial boundaries that help me keep my distance.

Here are few tips I've used that have been effective:

• I created a new email address for my daily use and didn't share the address with my ex. He only contacts me using my old account, which I check when I am ready. I no longer have his emails pushed to my phone.

• I changed his name in my phone to "Forgiveness," so if he calls or texts, his name doesn't suddenly pop up on my phone and trigger anxiety in the middle of my day. Yes, I know that it is him calling, but I am immediately reminded to think differently.

• I do not answer his phone calls as they come in and always let them go to voicemail. If there is something I need to respond to, then I do so by text or email, otherwise, I ignore them.

• I no longer respond to every accusation that populate his emails. I try to find the points I need to address, such as the kids' schedule, and only respond to that. If there is nothing in it about the kids that needs communication, then I don't respond at all.

• I no longer give him the right to share with me what he thinks of me. Oh, he still tries, but I've set a boundary against it. When his email offers some insight he thinks he has over me, I do my best to dismiss it. I divorced him. That means I don't want his "insights" about me anymore. I remind myself about that whenever he tries to get into my head.

• I have blocked him from my social media and never try to see his.

• I don't ask my children about their time with their dad. Instead, I ask broad questions like "How was your weekend?" Or I simply say, "I'm glad to see you!"

• I've asked my friends and family to avoid asking me questions about my ex. I have let them know that bringing up his name is painful for me and not simple chitchat.

• I've removed photos of us from my house.

Because my abuser is a nationally known sportswriter, at times it makes it hard to extract him from my daily life because he can suddenly pop up on TV, radio or the internet. A well-meaning family member or friend may ask about my ex because they are impressed with his job.

I've learned to deal with this as well.

I no longer pay much attention to the NFL, or watch football games, and accept that to do so means entering a world where my ex dwells. At first I was resentful about this. I have been a lifelong fan of professional football and I felt like I was giving up something to my abuser by staying away. I no longer feel that way. Instead, I see the NFL as a haven for abusers and a world I would rather not support. What was I really giving up?

I am more interested in filling my life now with things that don't remind me of my abusive ex-husband and instead help me feel grateful to be out of that sick marriage.

As my children have grown, it has become easier and easier.

Step 7

Help Your Children

As you move through the healing process and set boundaries to protect yourself, you will begin to feel better and get your mojo back. You may never shake the sadness that your children have been denied the perfect childhood you hoped for them.

Healthy parents want the best for their children. We may be involved in a terrible dynamic with our exes, but never lose sight of the reason you are reading this, to be the best parent you can be for your innocent children.

Since you have read to this point, I know that you are desperately trying to figure out a way to achieve that for your own kids despite your abusive ex.

Raising children isn't easy in the best of circumstances, with two loving and emotionally healthy parents. Raising children in an abusive home, during a custody battle or with a toxic ex, seems nearly impossible.

But, it can be done.

I find that my children really only need from me unconditional love and understanding. The rest is not as nearly as important. I don't have to be perfect or better or without mistakes for my children to understand these primary concepts: I am their mother; I love them and will never stop; we are a family and always will be; and nothing can change that. I let them know that over and over.

As my children weave their way through adolescence and early adulthood, I am here for them with acceptance and love even if they are struggling with the other relationships in their lives.

I write about this subject today so that I can be a better mother and because good emotional health is so important for our children. We know, even if no one else understands, that our children have a unique challenge in their lives because they have a parent who abused the other.

I don't spend a lot of time talking with my children about this, but when it is appropriate, I do.

Here is what I want my children to know:
- You are not the reason for the divorce.
- You are not the reason for the abuse.
- You are innocent.

- You are loved deeply.
- I have empathy for the unique walk you have juggling the various feelings you have about your parents' relationship.
- You are not hurting me if you love us both.
- You are not being disloyal if you want to spend time with your dad.
- I miss you when you are gone, but I am glad for you that you get to spend time with your dad.
- I will always understand your need to have a relationship with both your parents.
- I will always understand if you are struggling in your relationship with your parents.
- It sucks sometimes to have divorced parents.
- Forced togetherness with both your parents isn't always a good thing.
- You will always have a voice I want to hear, though I may not allow you to make a decision.
- I will always work to do the best for you, make the best decisions I can for you.
- I will make mistakes, but that doesn't mean I wanted to.
- I will say I'm sorry when I'm wrong.
- I will ask for your forgiveness if I mess up.
- I will also forgive your mess ups, too.

When I am taking care of myself emotionally and physically, I am best able to take care of my children. I can't state enough the importance of therapy in this effort. Before I was diagnosed with PTSD, I knew that my reactions to things were off. I didn't feel like myself and I was hurting. I was stressed and anxious about what might be coming around the corner. Raising two children as a single mother isn't easy, but doing so with anxiety makes it so much harder.

I could see that my once confident parenting style was fading fast and I was more and more unsure of myself as a parent. I needed help.

I found Jessica at that time in my life and I think I said to her in the first session so many years ago that I wanted to heal so I could be a better parent.

My emotional health was essential to my children's childhood, that much I knew.

It was the first step I knew in helping my kids deal with enormous change in their young lives. We couldn't all be a mess and make it.

At times, my life has been utterly exhausting. I describe it frequently as treading water in a turbulent ocean, carrying my kids on my shoulders as I try to get us to shore. The day that my older son graduated high school, I had the unbelievable sense of relief as I watched him in his cap and gown walk across the stage. I did it, I thought. He is OK.

Of course, my son still needs his mother despite being an adult and I still want him to know all those things I wrote above. I will always be there for my children.

I won't be able to stop things or people from hurting them, or turn back the clock and give them a different life. I can only accept that their experience, like everyone else, isn't perfect and they have challenges that most kids don't.

I see my children gracefully accept this too. They really don't complain about their circumstance or childhood. Like me, they will likely be dealing with childhood events for their entire lives. I sure hope not, but it would make them normal if it did.

Rather than dwell too long on the fantasy lost, I try to focus on the good and teach them tools to use when trauma and pain enter their worlds.

When appropriate:
- I have taught my children about therapy and why it's important.
- I have taught my children about domestic abuse and why it's not acceptable.
- I have taught my children to set boundaries in relationships.
- I have taught my children how to say they're sorry.
- I have taught my children about family and why it's important.

There is so much we teach our children from tying shoes to brushing teeth to saying please and thank you.

When you are co-parenting with an abuser, your children need extra lessons about life. They need you.

You may not be able to completely protect them from abuse, but you can be there for them if it happens and help them manage the pain and trauma they feel.

Don't ever let anyone tell you that you are not important to your kids. You are crucial.

Step 8

Be the Parent You Want to Be

I left my abusive husband and father of my children because I believed that giving my children a divorce instead the continued volatile home was the lesser of two evils. I was heartbroken that I couldn't figure out a way to give my children a healthy childhood that included both parents in the same home. I was a child of divorce and I knew that it wasn't an easy walk, especially when parents re-marry or they don't work well together after the break up.

I stayed with my abuser for many years even after I started to come out of the fog of denial because I clung to the last thread of hope that my children could be spared the repercussions of divorce. It was the absolute last thing I wanted for my kids.

When I made the decision to leave, I tried to set up an exit for myself and my children that was based in safety and the best hope for all of us to live better. I didn't feel any anger toward my husband or wish him ill. In fact, I knew that leaving him would cause him pain, deep pain. I assumed that our divorce would rip into his insecurities and damaged heart. I didn't want to do that to him. I just wanted to end the horrible turmoil domestic violence had caused in all of our lives.

So, when I filed for divorce, I did not hire the first bull-dog attorney. Instead, I hired a low-key divorce lawyer and tried to keep the terms simple. We sold our home and paid off our debt with the proceeds. We divided our things without any disagreement and split with our own retirement accounts and cars. We also agreed that I would move away with the children, to a town where our kids would get an excellent, public education and the cost of living was less.

I did all of this amicably because I knew that to enter a war with the father of my children was not good for anyone. As I've written, my husband was a nationally known sportswriter covering the NFL. I knew that if I followed the legal advice from the bull-dog attorney to publicly exposed the abuse, my children would be deeply hurt. My husband may have lost his job and even his career. I couldn't bare the thought that my children would be further disappointed and harmed or that he could lose everything.

I moved forward without any drama but I did want, and got, full custody of our children. He would have "liberal" visitation. I also maintained the role of primary parent in decision-making and record-keeping and the children's schedule.

It was very important to me because I knew, after living for 15 years with an abuser, if my husband had an equal say in anything, he would have opportunities to continue the power and control game with me and that could drive too many of his decisions.

I innately knew that in order for me and the children to truly be free from the abusive dynamic, he and I could not share daily parenting responsibilities. However, I also believed completely that my children needed and wanted to have their dad in their lives. I had no desire to keep my husband from seeing our children and I had zero thoughts of hate or revenge toward him. If anything, I felt sorry for him. He was about to lose his family and that broke my heart.

At the time, my husband didn't make a single case against my proposed arrangement. He didn't hire an attorney or come to court the day our divorce was made final. He didn't pay for any legal fees. I paid for it all and he didn't show any emotion beyond his initial reaction when I first told him that I wanted out. He did spend about six months apologizing to me for the abuses in our marriage and told me often that I was not to blame for the divorce.

I believed at the time that I was out from under the thumb of an abuser and my children would begin a new childhood free of the trauma of an abusive household. I knew they were sad and would miss their dad, but I knew it was better for all four of us.

Getting divorced was absolutely the most painful and difficult thing I had ever done. I still can't believe I was able to face the fear of it. I did it for my children's sanity as much as mine.

In the first five years of our divorce, my relationship with my ex-husband was difficult, but compared to what followed in the years after, it was a cake-walk.

When family law was rewritten in my state to make 50/50 shared time the standard, my ex found a way back into my life by suing for custody of our teenagers. He claimed I was preventing him from seeing our children, being involved in their lives and alienating him.

The day before I was served, I had been at my ex-husband's home for a pick-up and spent a few hours visiting with my him talking about our lives and latest work dramas. Just chatting and connecting as if nothing was wrong.

The next day my attorney called me to tell me she had just been served the documents laying out in more than 20 pages his complaints against me and his new demands. The day before at his home, he never said a word. I was completely blindsided.

Worse, I was traumatized all over again.

I always knew he was capable of causing me deep pain, but I had blamed his violence and abusive ways to an "overreaction" to an arguments and more spontaneous than premeditated. The custody suit was clearly a thoughtful process that required sitting down with an attorney and hammering out all the allegations and demands. He had to write a check for a retainer. Who knows what else was involved in this process, but it was no knee jerk reaction.

Further, I didn't know he was even upset with the current arrangement or that he thought I was alienating him. In fact, my ex-husband had always told me that I was an excellent mother and he was glad that my children had me. In all the years of beating, fighting and abuse, my treatment of our children or of him as their father was never the cause of a single incident.

He had in anger, many times, threatened me with a custody suit or that he would take away the children, but I chalked that up time and time again to his violent antics rather than an eventuality. As a result, when he followed through on his threat, I was completely shocked and baffled in a dramatic way.

However, where I once blamed myself for getting hit because I was a smart-mouth or unwilling to bend to my husband's will, I could not fathom what I had done to this man to cause such a hateful and hurtful action.

In the five years we had been divorced, he had weekly, overnight, unsupervised visitation. He was invited to birthday parties, school conferences, sporting events, and on and on.

We even coached our son's basketball team together two years in a row because my ex-husband asked me to help him with the task. When he decided a year after our divorce, that he wanted to move to our new town, I helped him find a house and set up our children's rooms and decorate his house.

Of course, all of this interaction with my abuser made me nervous and often I overcame anxiety to even be around him, but I thought at the time that is was best for our children for me to include him and work together.

In light of that, I couldn't believe how any attorney would take this case filled with so many false and unfounded accusations. This was just wrong and I told my attorney that this needed to be dismissed immediately.

Unfortunately, family court in my state doesn't work that way. Most motions filed by one parent against another, no matter the evidence, get it's day in court.

She told me that even though the evidence didn't support his accusations, or our children's successful lives, or his history of domestic abuse, we would have to tackle this all the way.

As her words washed over me, I was stunned. Quickly, I began to think about my children and how they would manage this. I had wanted so desperately for their childhoods to be better than this. First, they had to endure the horrors of an abusive household, then a divorce, now their father is suing their mother. My heart ached.

I was also an emotional mess. I couldn't accept that my children, who were now becoming more involved in their own lives, would have to deal with this. My oldest was about to enter an incredibly tough academic school year that was going to be challenging enough, without the drama of a family custody suit. I couldn't even think about the possible end result of losing custody.

Nothing about this made sense. I knew that my children were about to be deeply hurt on many levels. But, I couldn't stop it. Like so many times when my abuser beat me, he had sent us all over a cliff. We were now in free-fall.

My attorney described the suit and what was going to happen next. She said, under no circumstances was I to talk about this suit with my ex-husband. I was in a legal process under the control of our judicial system, she said. If I tried to handle this on my own with my ex, I could harm my standings with the court and my children's custody would be in jeopardy. I wanted to call my ex-husband right away and talk through this before it got out of hand and our children were really hurt. I wanted to stop the train wreck that was about to happen to them. She said, "Absolutely not."

I had been here so many times before. When my husband beat me, it almost always included my pleas for him to stop so that we could have a happy life together. I always was the one who searched for him after an incident and begged him to apologize for the abuse. I set up marriage counseling over and over. I tried to "teach" him how to show me remorse for his abusive actions. I wanted so desperately for us to stay together. My denial was so invasive.

Our dynamic followed the same pattern: an argument that escalated into a fight; destructive, unthinkable abuse; separation that lasted a few hours to a few weeks; then I would reach out to him and ask him to reconcile; finally, analysis of what went wrong.

We would then re-engage in a more normal life as if the event never happened. This cycle continued over and over. https://en.wikipedia.org/wiki/Cycle_of_abuse

The minute I heard he had filed a custody suit, I desperately wanted to go to that comfort zone. I believed that was the only hope of getting back to normal for all of us.

Our legal system doesn't allow for this dynamic and maybe that is a good thing. I'm still not sure. What this new dynamic did do, was give my ex-husband a clear path to grab power and control over his long-time victim and in the process hand over parenting of our well-adjusted children to strangers in a family court. I attempted more than once to offer settlements I thought would save my children from the horrors of a custody suit and would give them a manageable daily life. If my ex-husband won the custody suit, then my children's lives would be incredibly hard for them to management and I wanted to save them from that.

I did everything I could to bury my own hurt and pain and poured all my focus into getting a custody plan that wouldn't hurt my kids. I spent eight months collecting evidence, getting letters from loved-ones and friends about my parenting and the kids. I wanted to be prepared to fight to keep their school weeks normal and as much of their daily lives the same. I no longer cared about maintaining sole parenting decisions and let that go immediately. I didn't want my children to make constant switches from house to house and live out of a suitcase. That seemed unbearable.

I also didn't want my children to be forced to become part of a "new" family that my ex was forming with a new wife and stepchild. I knew my kids were struggling with this and needed time to adjust. It appeared to me that his wife was not appreciating this and instead was driving the custody case for their own cause.

As heartbroken and scared as I watched my children's fate get turned over to strangers, I knew I had to stay strong and work out the problem. It took an enormous toll on me emotionally.

In the end, my ex finally agreed to a settlement that gave him only slightly more visitation than he already had but he gained joint parenting decision-making. We were now "co-parenting" in the eyes of the court and even with a very detailed parenting plan, this new dynamic gave my abuser many opportunities to exert coercive control over us and he did.

There is no way my children's lives were better through the eight months of hell the custody suit put us through. It stripped away their confident, calm mother, their security and their safety. It gave them many months of uncertainly for their future. I knew the day I was served that my children's mental health was going to be damaged by this. My children, who were thriving in life, were not seeking a change to their daily lives. Suddenly, they were forced into a state of limbo and wait for a civil suit to decide their fate. I couldn't believe my ex-husband could do something like this to our babies.

Since I've lived through both worlds of custody arrangements, I have seen the results of each. I believe completely that my children were better off with the non-abusive parent in control of decisions and schedules. Abusers by their very nature want to win, control and have power over people. Giving them joint custody just gives them a constant source of opportunity to dominate and it is often at the detriment of the kids.

Co-parenting with a toxic ex is very difficult. There are overt and subtle ways that an abuser attempts to gain and maintain power, control and intimidate their victims. Too many people assume that if you are not getting hit, then you are not a victim of domestic abuse. Nothing could be further from the truth.

Trying to be the best parent in the face of on-going abuse is challenging and confusing. I often knew that my parenting decisions were tainted by the trauma of abuse. I sometimes made decisions because I was reacting to the undercurrent of fear of my abuser, my co-parent.

I am thankful that when the judicial system failed my family by putting us back in harm's way, the domestic abuse community was there for us. I went back to my domestic abuse center and asked for help and got it. That is where I found Jessica and where the healing has taken place ever since. Without emotional healing, I doubt I would have been able to recover enough to parent my children well after the trauma of a frivolously custody suit.

Today, my children are basically grown and their needs have changed in many ways. I am able to get back to my core values as a person and a parent when dealing with my children. I focus on expressing what I value instead of trying not to piss off "the system." I used to fear that if I made a bad or incorrect parenting decision, then I would lose custody of my kids. Thankfully, all of my research and therapy has helped me to focus on something better. I've learned that no matter what, I am my children's mother and they need me. No court in the land, or abusive jerk, can change that.

I value that role so much and see it as a enormous responsibility. I owe my children my best. Taking care of myself emotionally, helps me take care of my children. I know that each day with an abuser in our lives comes with a brand new challenge that may not make sense or seems necessary. There are no laws or agencies that can completely stop my ex-husband from abusing me or my children. He is the only person able to do that and he hasn't shown a willingness to so far.

So instead, I know that our daily lives are uncertain. There is not a game plan or "correct" way of behaving that I can implement that will give us a clear path away from an abuser. I must be at my best in order to handle that challenge that we know can come, when you are connected to an abuser.

I often receive requests from victims of abuse who are co-parenting with an abuser for advice on how to manage a latest court motion or incident they have experienced at the hands of their abuser. This book came to be because of the lack of information available for those forced to co-parent with their toxic ex. I have coached people as best I can. I'm no expert, just a victim who has been through it and done a lot of research. When asked for advice, I almost always tell women to proceed with their children's best interest in mind, with caution and concern for safety.

Because each state has different laws and each community has different attorneys and judges, there is no telling what will happen to victims in family court today. I don't believe that abusers should ever co-parent with their victims, because it is not in the best interest of children. Go back and read my message at the beginning of this book to be reminded why. However, there are plenty of judges out there who feel differently.

Children need security and stability above all and forcing a victim to stay in almost daily communication with their abuser, will only make her less able to provide that for her kids. And yet, courts around the land not only expect the victims to perform at their best, they also insist on dismissing the victim's fear and pain while requiring nothing of the abuser.

It is unfair and idiotic, but it is common.

You, the victim who is parenting with your abuser, somehow and despite this unfairness, have to find a way to keep your sanity because your children need you more than ever.

Parenting studies have shown that a child needs only one emotionally stable parent to grow up healthy. You are the only parent in their lives who can hope to achieve that goal. An abuser is not emotionally healthy and their choice to abuse is proof of that. Remember, it doesn't take two to tango in domestic abuse. It takes just one abuser. When you remove the abuser, you remove the abuse.

My hope for you and your kids is that you can navigate the crap that he will throw at you during your time co-parenting because when you are down, your children suffer.

Also, don't be too hard on yourself when you can't manage your best. Instead, let your kids know when you are sorry for any actions you regret and are sorry that they are in this mess. Let them know that you are trying your best and still have expectations and dreams.

Understand when your kids are upset, confused or feel guilty. Children are not born to understand this and society doesn't train us to handle abuse.

Your children want to believe in both parents and want to love them. They also want to know that their parents love them and are proud. Unfortunately, abusers often get this wrong. Too often, children of abuse feel shame because of how their abusive parent treats them. Just like us.

The fantasy that kept you in the marriage is a similar fantasy that children have about their parents and their home. They often wish for what can't be. Help your kids through this with understanding and time. Don't expect your children to understand your journey. They may never truly grasp what you went through.

Don't try to force your child to see the horrors that your ex has caused you. Don't try to win their support. Don't try to pit yourself against your ex. And don't fault your child for having conflicting feelings about both of you.

Over time, your child will come to understand their playing field. If you can stay out of the daily anxiety you rightfully have about your children's health and your fears about your ex, then you can build a relationship with your kids that is solid and healthy.

Build trust with your kids. They need it and won't likely get it from their abusive parent.

Don't lie to them. Don't tell them things you don't mean. Don't try to "parent out" the traits you see in them that remind you of your ex. They are not abusers and they won't become one because, they have you.

Don't worry when your teenagers become little narcissists. All teenagers go through that developmental stage and it's normal. Manage the ups and downs of that parenting stage with as much calm and acceptance that you can muster. And tell them you're sorry when you fail.

All of this is very difficult. You will always need to apply a lot of effort in other parts of your life in order to stay as grounded in your own values as a parent. But, you won't be perfect and wouldn't be even if abuse was never in your life.

After all of my research, life experience and mistakes, I have come to understand that I want my children to really know me, warts and all. I have tried my best to give them everything they need. I want them to know that life's a journey, often difficult and very unfair, but it is also wonderful.

I try to teach them how to help others and forgive those who hurt us. But, I also tell them they are in charge of establishing their own boundaries against abuse. In my house, they are allowed to feel at home and relaxed. An abuser can often take up all the space in a room. I want them to have a place in my home that doesn't feel like that.

My abuser's post-divorce actions have rocked me many times in traumatic ways. Living with PTSD triggered by a custody suit really affected my parenting.

Coming through that because of excellent therapy gave me my parenting confidence back. I know that some people might make different parenting choices, but I'm good with the ones I make for my children. Thankfully, I am able to make decisions in parenting that are based in what I believe is right for my kids. I no longer base my parenting on what I think a judge will think or if my ex will react badly.

I used my own values system and what I think is best. I don't give people who don't know my children personally, a say in how I parenting them beyond just listening to their educated advice. When I was really suffering, even a friend's comment about a parenting choice I made would send me into doubts about what I did. I was afraid that any wrong move would jeopardize my kids' custody. Not anymore.

Getting emotionally healthy has given me and my kids the best gift through this horrible journey.

A female victim co-parenting with her abuser called me one day in a panic because her ex was doing his best to drive a wedge between her teenage daughter and her. She was scared to death of what could happen. She told me that it had gotten so bad, that one day that week here her daughter was home alone, grounded for violating her mother's curfew rule. Her daughter called her father to complain, and he told the teenager to get packed because he was coming to get her and save her from her "ruthless" mother's punishment. When he pulled into my friend's driveway, her daughter didn't leave. Instead, she walked out to the car and told her dad to go home. She was staying put.

As she told me the story, I smiled. That moment proved that this woman had already instilled in her daughter her values. Her daughter wouldn't break her punishment even though her father told her she could. This woman's ex had tried to break the bond between them, but it didn't work. Her 14-year-old daughter clearly valued her mother's opinion and trusted her.

I told her she was a great mom and to keep parenting the way that she thinks its best. Teenagers will try your patiences, and test the boundaries and make you feel crazy. But, they are supposed to. Stay the course and let your kids know that you love them through the ups and downs.

In my experience, when I'm emotionally healthy, I can feel in my heart my values and core parenting beliefs. When I do, I offer my children my best. No court or abuser or stranger on the street can ever tell me how I am *supposed* to feel about my children or what I think is right for them. They may tell me I'm wrong, have another opinion or take away my ability to implement my parenting beliefs, but what's in my heart and head is mine. I want my children to know what I think is best for them, because after all, I am their mother.

Abusers and uninformed family court officers may have the ability to reduce your time with your children, change your household structure or cause you daily challenges in your parenting, but they can not take away the fact that you are your child's parent and you have a relationship that is just between the two of you.

Recently, my sister was on a business trip that enabled her to meet up with my college-student son for dinner. Despite living far apart, they have a close relationship and they were both happy to see each other. After dinner, they each called me to tell me how much fun they had and how nice it was to be together. I was happy for them both and glad that my son had his aunt there to visit.

But, I got another unexpected gift that night. My sister, who knows all about my journey parenting with my abuser, shared with me something she knew would mean a lot. She told me that throughout the night of various stories, my son spoke very highly of me and with respect. My son and I had been going through a several minor challenges with the outside world together and he told my sister about these incidents. He told her how hard I worked and how steadfast I was as we faced these incidents together. She told me, "Sis, he really respects you." I was in tears and thankful.

I had realized at that moment that my relationship with my son was solid no matter what we had been through or no matter how my abusive ex had negatively influenced our relationship. My son respected his mom and that was exactly what I wanted for my children. I believe that when children have faith in a parent, they start their lives on solid ground.

I will be forever grateful that I had the opportunity after divorce to parent my children absent of the abuse we once daily had in our home. Despite divorce, it was still very hard to keep domestic abuse out of my house. But, I did it. First, by leaving my ex; then getting the emotional help I needed to heal; and finally, getting the legal help I needed to set as many boundaries as I could. Because of those steps, I was able to parent my children most of the time the way I believed was in their best interest.

I can't imagine what it would have been like for them if I had stayed in that marriage, but I don't think their childhoods would have ended as happily as my sister's dinner that night.

I urge you to process the abuse you face. If you do, you can find peace in parenting and guide your children as you see fit. You are their parent and that means the world to them. Don't ever forget that or believe anyone who tells you that you are wrong for taking seriously the responsibility.

Your New Life

Living with the New Normal

No one would ever choose to co-parent with their abuser. It is so idiotic that people unfamiliar with abuse just assume this isn't done. Recently, I was interviewed for a local TV news show about domestic abuse. The reporter changed the entire piece when she discovered I was co-parenting with my abuser. She couldn't believe I was forced to co-parent with the man who beat me up. She just assumed that when there is proven domestic violence, the victim gets to leave with the children and never look back.

She was shocked and asked me the most basic questions, like "How are you doing this?"

Once, I was that amazed, too. Then reality set in and I began to understand the playing field.

Through research and interviews with victims, social media contacts and therapy, I've come to accept the new normal in child custody and divorce. I've lived through both standards of custody arrangements and found that co-parenting only empowers abusers and hurts victims and children. The research supports this as well. However, when we can't control the circumstances, it's best to find emotional peace. When we argue, fight and demand the unfair treatment stop, we end up looking like hysterical women more concerned with our own feelings to those who have the power to judge us. Our abusers often sit back and smile knowing we played right into their hands.

Further, I have seen victims of abuse turn so bitter and reactive to victim-blaming and shaming that they are no longer liked by family and friends or trusted by their children. Though it is completely understandable for these strong emotions to develop in victims, their behavior is often used against them.

Like the adage: Holding onto anger toward those you hurt you is like taking poison and expecting the other person to get sick. It just doesn't work. It would, of course, be fair. Abusers should be forced to give back the stolen years to their families or change the history. But, they can't.

Only we victims can take the steps necessary to heal our wounds. I don't recommend trying to go it alone nor do I much care for flip comments like "Just get over it." It takes time, real effort and excellent therapy to properly treat the emotional damage of abuse. Rather than take poison to get back at your ex, try taking medicine to heal your pain. It will work and you will move past it if you do.

I have told people that a domestic abuse victim often feels like they just stepped off a curve and got hit by a bus. While the poor, bleeding victim is lying on the road, broken and in pain, the passers-by stop to ask, "Why didn't you look both ways." No one rushes her to the hospital or brings her flowers. Too few professionals know how to fix her wounds. So, she has to limp around with bones that never set and wounds that were never treated. And she blames herself for stepping off the curve in the first place.

No one would ever treat an accident victim like that, yet abuse victims are treated that way every day. We domestic abuse victims are just as innocent as that person who forgot to look both ways and got hit by a bus.

I believe that times will change. The biases in the courts will shift. More and more studies will come out showing the damage this is doing to people. One day, this type of book won't be necessary. In the meantime, I hope you all know that you can survive this just like you survived the abuse in your home. You need to always stay aware of safety and danger.

I am very sorry that you are facing this and that your children are growing up with this challenge.

I know that you can navigate it and can get to the other side with much of yourself in tact. Reach out to others. Share your story. Don't try to go it alone. Most importantly, cling to the happy moments with your children as much as possible. It all goes by so fast.

About the Author

Julie Boyd Cole is a mother, writer, journalist and domestic abuse survivor. She grew up in upstate New York and now lives in Florida. She has worked for the Miami Herald, the Fort Lauderdale Sun-Sentinel, newspapers in the suburbs of San Francisco, Washington, D.C. and written for yahoo.com, divorcedmoms.com, goodmenproject.com and stopabusecampaign.com. She also writes for bruisedwomen.com and *@bruisedwoman* on Twitter.

Julie survived a 15-year relationship with an abuser, who first physically assaulted her when she was nine months pregnant, when he tried to strangle her. She lived the next 10 years getting beaten repeatedly, among other emotional and psychological abuses until finally she decided to leave with her children.

After five years of having full custody of her children, the laws in her state changed that allowed her ex-husband to sue her for custody. In an eight-month legal action over the custody of her teenagers, Julie was diagnosed with PTSD.

Julie's journey was made worse by her ex-husband's modest fame as an NFL national sports writer and the lack of accountability placed on people with power and money.

She began to study and research domestic abuse soon after she divorced her abuser as a way to heal from the trauma. Through work with Peaceful Paths, a domestic abuse center in North Central Florida, and trauma treatment therapy with Jessica Goldberg of the *Center for Balance*, she has been successfully treated.

She now is the facilitator of YANA Support Group and an online support group that draws in victims from all over the world.

To reach Julie, please email her at julieboydcole@gmail.com

Resources

There are a few of the resources used in this book and may help you in your journey:

Three authors worth reading to help you understand domestic abuse and co-parenting:
Lundy Bancroft, "When Dad Hurts Mom"
Barry Goldstein, (http://www.barrygoldstein.net/books/domestic-violence-abuse-and-child-custody)
Cathy Meyer, Editor of divorcedmoms.com

Legal opinions that support victims in custody cases:
http://stopabusecampaign.com/the-quincy-solution/

PDF of guidelines from the Institute of Safe Families:
http://www.instituteforsafefamilies.org/sites/default/files/isfFiles/Parenting-After-Violence.pdf

Department of Justice definition of domestic abuse:
http://www.justice.gov/ovw/domestic-violence

My articles on divorcedmoms.com:
http://divorcedmoms.com/blogs/thriving-in-crazy-land

How we got here:
http://americannewsreport.com/joint-child-custody-co-parenting-divorce-8821356

Child Custody Legal expert Barry Goldberg:
http://www.barrygoldstein.net/important-articles/shared-custody

2006 study on dynamics of child custody and domestic abuse:
http://faculty.spokanefalls.edu/InetShare/AutoWebs/kimt/co-parenting%20with%20abusive.pdf

Post Traumatic Stress Disorder information:
http://www.ptsd.va.gov/public/types/violence/domestic-violence.asp

The results of my 2015 survey of domestic abuse victims and co-parenting:
https://drive.google.com/file/d/0B-8SRf8TQffZMlVjdkJMbklsR0k/view?usp=sharing

U.S. National Coalition Against Domestic Violence definition of abuse:
http://www.ncadv.org/need-help/what-is-domestic-violence
For Safety information and excellent tips of managing a domestic abuse situation:
http://www.thehotline.org/

Made in the USA
Columbia, SC
10 July 2017